GARLAND STUDIES ON

# INDUSTRIAL PRODUCTIVITY

*edited by*

**STUART BRUCHEY**
UNIVERSITY OF MAINE

A GARLAND SERIES

# IMMIGRANT LINKS TO THE HOME COUNTRY

## IMPLICATIONS FOR TRADE, WELFARE, AND FACTOR RETURNS

DAVID GOULD

GARLAND PUBLISHING, INC.
NEW YORK & LONDON / 1996

**Library of Congress Cataloging-in-Publication Data**

Gould, David.
    Immigrant links to the home country : Implications for trade,
welfare, and factor returns / David Gould.
        p.    cm. — (Garland studies on industrial productivity )
    Includes bibliographical references and index.
    ISBN 0-8153-2441-3 (alk. paper)
    1. California—Commerce—Mexico. 2. Mexico—Commerce—
California. 3. Mexican Americans—California—Commerce.
4. California—Emigration and immigration—Economic aspects.
5. Income—California. 6. Wages—California. I. Title. II. Series.
HF3161.C2G68 1996
382'.09720794—dc20                                        95-53022

Printed on acid-free, 250-year-life paper
Manufactured in the United States of America

For Robin

# Contents

# Figures and Tables

Figures

Tables

# Preface

Immigration appears to be taking center stage in an increasing number of issues. One of the most heated arguments during the North American Free Trade Agreement (NAFTA) debate was whether freer trade with Mexico was going to increase or decrease the tide of Mexican immigrants coming to the United States. California's Proposition 187 was enacted out of fears that the enormous flow of illegal immigration into California was putting an undue strain on social services and the economy. Whether or not immigration fears are justified, they do represent a growing perception that immigration has become harmful to the country and that something should be done to change U.S. immigration policy.

This volume contains new and substantially updated research from my doctoral dissertation at the University of California, Los Angeles. While studying and living in Los Angeles during the late 1980s, I realized that the debates over immigration did not account for all the effects of immigration that I was observing. I became interested in the arguments about immigration and also sensitized to the economic impact that immigrants might have on a community. Perhaps there is no other place in the world where the effects of immigration are more evident than in Los Angeles. It is estimated that over 30 percent of the Los Angeles population is foreign-born, and most of these immigrants arrived during the last two decades. It is in this type of environment that the effects of immigration are most observable.

Although the economics literature had delved quite extensively into how immigrants might influence wages and income in a host country, one influence of immigration that became rapidly apparent to me in Los Angeles, but was not discussed in the literature, was the impact immigrants had on the type and quantity of foreign goods available. Not only were immigrants consuming goods from their own home countries, but natives (including myself) were being exposed to these goods as well and, in some cases, developing a preference for them. Another aspect of immigration that came to my attention was the number of individuals from the various immigrant communities who were involved in trading activities with their home countries. These individuals were importing goods from their home countries for consumption by the local immigrant community, but they were also exporting goods from the United States to their home countries. During the late 1980s, China was beginning to dramatically open up commerce to the rest of the world. Some of the first U.S. entrepreneurs to develop trading relationships with China were Chinese immigrants to the United States who had arrived decades earlier. There are numerous other examples of this phenomenon across immigrant communities and countries.

I call these ties and trading relationships that develop between the host and home countries immigrant links to the home country. In this book, I provide evidence that immigrant links can have an important impact on the host country's trade, income, and wages.

The research in this book owes a great debt to my dissertation advisor, Professor Edward Leamer, who encouraged me to pursue this somewhat risky and uncharted research agenda. I have also benefited from numerous discussions with Sebastian Edwards, Bruce Chelimsky Fallick, John K. Hill, Thomas B. Fomby, Miguel A. Savastano, Graeme Woodbridge, Roy Ruffin, John V. Duca, and W. Michael Cox. Rhonda Harris provided excellent editorial assistance.

Finally, I owe much to my family. My deepest debt is to my wife, Robin, whose love and support have been my light.

Dallas, Texas
November 1995

# Immigrant Links
# to the Home Country

# Chapter 1

# Introduction

In recent years, the world has experienced some of the largest increases in the international migration of people since the turn of the century. In 1990, the U.S. census recorded more than 19.7 million foreign-born residents, 29 percent of whom immigrated between 1980 and 1990. This is one of the highest intercensal increases in foreign-born population in U.S. history, representing 27 percent of the increment in population.[1] In Canada, low native fertility rates, combined with new liberal immigration policies, resulted in immigration that accounted for 33 percent of the increment in population between 1966 and 1975, and 36 percent in 1977.[2] The West German *gastarbeiter*, or "guestworker," system of immigration encouraged a large inflow of foreign labor, mainly from the former Yugoslavia, Turkey, Greece, Italy, Portugal, and Spain. From 1961 to 1979, the foreign population in West Germany increased from 686,000 to 4.1 million, representing 66 percent of the total increment in population. Recent political and economic turmoil in Latin America, the former Soviet Union, and Eastern European countries has led to large emigration pressures and suggests that migration will continue to be an extremely important economic force in the years to come.

Along with these recent increases in immigration levels there has been a continuing debate in many countries with liberal immigration laws—such as Canada, Australia, and the United States—about the consequences of the current levels of immigration and the changing source country distribution of immigration. Some groups within these source countries claim that immigrants are taking jobs away from natives, are putting increased stress on limited resources, and are placing an additional burden on already over-burdened social service systems. On the other hand, recent polling data in Southern California, where new immigrant communities are concentrated, suggest that natives do not see themselves as being in competition with immigrants for jobs or social services. Natives do, however, see such people as a general threat to their quality of life due to cultural differences, fears of a multi-lingual society, and overcrowding.[3]

In the United States, ethnic diversity in the flow of immigrants is one of the key issues of debate in current immigration reform discussions. The concern is that access to the United States by nationals of the traditional source countries of U.S. immigration has been hampered as an unintended consequence of U.S. immigration policy. In the present system, immediate family members of U.S. citizens are exempt from numerical limitations on immigration, and other close family members are given priority in the over-all numerically limited preference categories. So, if a country has a high present level of immigration, future immigration will also be high as family members are carried over on a previous immigrant's visa. Consequently, current immigration policy has created a system in which a country's future immigrants will be pushed aside by immigrants from other higher visa-demand countries unless a country's demand for immigrant visas remains stable relative to that of other countries.[4] Nationals of only six countries accounted for 55 percent of all visas issued by the United States between 1986 and 1990.[5] Similar concerns have been voiced in other countries, such as West Germany, where the massive exodus of East Germans to the West pushed aside immigrants from Asian and Southern European countries.

While recent large flows of international labor migration have generated a substantial descriptive literature, the formal economic treatment has been rather limited.[6] Most formal economic models of immigration treat immigrants as indistinguishable from current residents. In these models, the primary difference between an increase in domestic labor and foreign labor is the treatment of national welfare (*i.e.*, Are immigrants included in the host country's welfare?) and the question of whether or not foreign labor is accompanied with physical as well as human capital.[7] Within the standard 2X2 Heckscher-Ohlin-Samuelson model of international trade, not even the returns to factors are affected by immigration because it only affects the composition of outputs, at least until the level of immigration is sufficient to induce the complete specialization of production in one of the goods.

The existing literature on immigration has implicitly assumed that the economic consequences of immigration are independent of the country or region in which the labor originates. In fact, the effects are equivalent to an additional supply of labor from the native population, so long as all other factors of production are held constant. This assumption, however, may ignore other important effects of immigration, such as the close ties or links immigrants maintain with their home countries. Moreover, immigrant links to the home country can have trade-enhancing effects for both the host and home countries. Immigrant links to the home country include the introduction into the host country of the immigrant's language, preferences, knowledge of home country markets, and contacts.

The question addressed in this book is the following: Do immigrant links to the home country affect the bilateral trade flows between the home and host countries? This is important in assessing the economic consequences of immigration as well understanding the political economy of immigration (*i.e.*, Who will lobby for immigration liberalizations or restrictions). Furthermore, questions concerning the changing source country distribution of immigrants can be addressed in this context. Does it make a difference to a host country whether it receives 100,000 immigrants from only one country or from a dozen different countries? Should a host country actively promote diversity in its immigration policy, or should it be passive?

Tables 1 through 3 show how the distribution of bilateral

Table 1

United States: Distribution of Foreign-Born Persons and Trade (In Percentages)

| Region | Immigrant Stock | | Trade | |
|--------|------|------|------|------|
|        | 1970 | 1990 | 1970 | 1990 |
| Europe | 54.8 | 23.8 | 32.5 | 25.6 |
| Asia   | 9.3  | 25   | 22.8 | 33.6 |
| Canada | 7.9  | 4    | 24.1 | 19.4 |
| Mexico | 8.0  | 20.6 | 4.2  | 6.5  |
| Other  | 20.0 | 26.6 | 18.4 | 14.9 |
| Total  | 100.0 | 100.0 | 100.0 | 100.0 |

Source: 1990 and 1970 U.S. Census and
the Direction of Trade Statistics

trade flows and the source country distribution of immigrant stocks changed during the 1970s and 1980s for the United States, Canada and Australia.[8] As can be seen, these three countries have experienced similar movements in immigration and bilateral trade flows. That is, as the distribution of immigrants has shifted away from traditional, European source countries to the non-traditional Latin American and Asian countries, the distribution of bilateral trade flows has shifted in a similar direction. As can be seen from the tables, the distributions of bilateral trade and immigrant stocks have mostly moved in the same directions.  The similar shifts in the distribution of immigrants for these countries reflect to a large degree the coincident changes in immigration policy experienced in these three countries. In 1965, amendments to U.S. immigration laws changed the principal criteria used to control entry into the United States from the national origin quotas, which had a bias against immigrants from Asian countries, to a system based on overall immigration limits with no limits for those claiming familial kinship with an American citizen or resident. Canadian law until 1962 extended preferential treatment to Northwestern European nations and restricted Asian immigration. This policy was

Table 2

Australia: Distribution of Foreign-Born Persons and Trade (In Percentages)

| Region | Immigrant Stock | | Trade | |
|---|---|---|---|---|
| | 1969 | 1991 | 1969 | 1991 |
| Europe | 87.4 | 61.4 | 34.0 | 20.0 |
| Asia | 3.2 | 18.1 | 33.6 | 48.5 |
| Canada/U.S. | 1.9 | 1.8 | 23.2 | 18.6 |
| Oceania | 2.8 | 9.4 | 4.0 | 7.1 |
| Latin America | 0.3 | 1.8 | 1.0 | 1.1 |
| Other | 3.9 | 7.2 | 4.2 | 4.7 |
| Total | 100.0 | 100.0 | 100.0 | 100.0 |

Source: Australian Consolidated Statistics, 1991 and the Direction of Trade Statistics

Table 3

Canada: Distribution of Foreign-Born Persons and Trade (In Percentages)

| Region | Immigrant Stock | | Trade | |
|---|---|---|---|---|
| | 1966 | 1991 | 1966 | 1991 |
| Europe | 87.3 | 54.4 | 18.5 | 11.8 |
| Asia | 3.9 | 24.5 | 5.9 | 12.1 |
| U.S. | 3.8 | 5.7 | 70.6 | 69.2 |
| Other | 4.4 | 15.3 | 5.0 | 6.9 |
| Total | 100.0 | 100.0 | 100.0 | 100.0 |

Source: Canada Census, 1991 and the Direction of Trade Statistics

similar to the U.S. national origin quota system. Australia followed the same pattern as the United States and Canada, with an immigration policy that favored European immigration until 1973. The liberalization of immigration policies in these countries has enabled similar and unprecedented influxes of immigrants from developing countries. However, each country has also had distinct immigration experiences. First, European, and particularly British, immigrants have remained more dominant in Canada and Australia than in the United States. Second, during the 1970s the ratio of immigrants to natives has remained the highest in Australia, with 19.3 percent; Canada second, with 18.5 percent; and the United States third, with 11.7 percent.[9] Finally, labor market considerations have played a greater role in immigration policy in Canada than in the United States or Australia. In 1974, the Canadian Parliament enacted legislation that favored immigrants with prearranged employment and needed skills.[10]

Although many factors may have contributed to the coincident movements in trade and immigration captured in these tables, the pattern suggests that immigrants may play a role in determining bilateral trade flows and motivates this study's investigation into the possible trade enhancing aspects of immigration. In particular, I postulate that immigrant links to the home country can have an important impact on bilateral trade flows between the host and home countries through the introduction into the host country of the immigrant's language, preferences, knowledge of home country markets, and contacts.

The mechanisms by which immigrant links influence bilateral trade flows may be sorted into two general categories. The first refers to immigrant preference for home country products, and the other refers to the transactions costs to trade associated with information and trust.

While the first class of mechanisms suggests that immigrants' consumption of their home country products will result in a direct increase in the host country's imports of these goods, the second is much broader in the sense that it predicts a direct increase in both export and import flows between the host and home countries through a decrease in transactions costs associated with obtaining foreign market information establishing trade relationships.

There are several ways in which the immigrant links can decrease the transactions costs to trade associated with foreign market information and developing trust. First, the native language of the immigrants can become known, or used more often, by the residents of the host country. This can create a larger group of individuals in the host country, immigrants and non-immigrants, who are bilingual in the languages of the host and home countries, which diminishes the trading costs due to communication barriers. Second, if products are differentiated across countries, and immigrants bring information about their home country products and preferences, the costs of obtaining this market information in the host country will decrease. Finally, because trade often depends on contracts for delivery and payment, the development of trust through immigrant contacts can decrease the costs associated with negotiating trade contracts and insuring their enforcement.

The importance of these factors, of course, would depend on the initial amount of foreign market information in the host country and the ability of immigrants to relay information and to integrate their communities into the host country.[11] This, in turn, may depend upon the educational level of the immigrants, the length of their stay in the host country, and the size of the immigrant community. The size of the community can be particularly important when looking at how changes in immigration influence transactions costs and trade. With a relatively small immigrant community, an increase in home country information via immigration may be unnoticeable. On the other hand, when the community is large, so much information is already available that additional immigration may not provide much new information or cause a decrease in transactions costs. Consequently, the decrease in transactions costs may not begin until a critical level in immigration is achieved, and then the rise may slow until all the information benefits are exhausted.

## 1.1  OVERVIEW

This book examines an aspect of international labor migration that has received little attention in the formal economic literature, that is, the close ties or links that an immigrant community maintains with its home country and the trade-enhancing effect this can have on bilateral trade flows between the host and home country. These trade-creating linkages to the home country can develop by the introduction into the host country of the immigrant's language, preferences, knowledge of home country markets, and contacts. This new information, or more easily obtainable information, can facilitate trade through a decrease in transactions costs and an increase in mutual trust between trading partners.

In chapter 2, I discuss the literature on immigration and trade. In chapter 3, I present a general equilibrium model of trade that incorporates the hypothesis that immigrants increase foreign market information and decrease the transactions costs to trade between the host and home countries. Within this model, I discuss the welfare, trade, and factor market implications of immigration and immigrant links. The assumptions of the model follow directly from the standard trade models discussed above, except that immigrants decrease the transactions costs of trade as well as change the factor endowments of the host country. As opposed to the models of immigration and trade presented above, the model developed here predicts that *bilateral* and *total* trade flows between the host and home countries will be directly influenced by immigration. Furthermore, welfare is increased as a result of immigration decreasing transactions costs.

In chapter 4, I develop a specific case of the general model as a framework to empirically examine the relationship between immigrant links and bilateral trade flows. In chapter 5, I present the empirical model, discuss data to be used in the analysis, and present the results of the empirical analysis. Data on immigration, immigrant characteristics, trade, prices, and incomes are collected and examined for the case of the United States.

The empirical analysis of chapter 5 contributes to the literature on immigration and trade in two ways. First, it utilizes immigration data of two destination countries to determine the relationship between immigration and trade flows. Second, it investigates the effects of immigrant links to the home country by looking at the relationship between immigration and bilateral trade flows for aggregate exports and imports, consumer-manufactured exports and imports, and producer-manufactured exports and imports. Finally, chapter 6 summarizes the findings of the book and discusses the economic consequences of various immigration policies.

# NOTES

[1] See Borjas (1990) for an analysis of the recent immigration.

[2] Keely and Elwell (1981).

[3] Cornelius (1990).

[4] Papademetriou (1990).

[5] These counties are, in descending order, Mexico, the Philippines, South Korea, the Dominican Republic, India, and China (mainland).

[6] For the descriptive literature see, for example, Greenwood (1983), Greenwood and McDowell (1985), and Reubens (1983).

[7] See Johnson (1967), Grubel and Scott (1966), Berry and Soligo (1969) and, Bhagwati and Rodriguez(1975). For a survey of the literature, see Ruffin (1984).

[8] The immigrant stock is is the total number of immigrants.

[9] Zubrzycki (1981).

[10] Keely and Elwell (1981).

[11] Certainly, immigration is not the only way a host country can obtain foreign market information. Immigration may, however, increase the availability of such information, which would decrease its marginal cost.

# Chapter 2

# Literature Review

The literature on immigration presents no formal analysis of immigrant links to the home country. However, the literature does offer some insights to help put the issue of immigrant links into context, in particular, the descriptive literature on immigrant networks and immigrant entrepreneurs, the literature on factor movements and trade, and the literature on immigration and welfare and factor returns. The review that follows will attempt to synthesize this literature as it applies to immigrant links to the home country.

## 2.1 IMMIGRANT NETWORKS AND ENTREPRENEURS

In describing migration flows, economists have typically looked to differences in wages as the single most important factor in determining where migrants locate. However, once a migrant has made the decision to relocate, to which higher wage country does he or she migrate? Obviously, the decision to migrate and where to migrate depends not only on the potential earnings but also on the travel costs, the psychic costs of traveling to a foreign land, and the costs of obtaining information about work and housing in the destination country.

In the last decade, immigration research, particularly in the sociology literature, has focused attention on the issue of immigrant networks in determining immigration flows and destination countries.[1] Immigrant networks are the family or friends of a particular ethnic or nationality group in a destination country that assists potential migrants in relocation. These networks organize the migrant's departure, travel, and settlement abroad. As immigrant networks mature, they can become a further impetus for migratory flows, and not just a result of them. According to Massey (1988), migrations forge networks that then facilitate the very migrations that produced them. Therefore, whatever economic conditions may initially have caused migration, the expanding migratory process can become "progressively independent" of the original causal conditions.[2] Massey (1988) defined migration networks in a broad sense as "sets of interpersonal ties that link migrants, former migrants, and non-migrants in origin and destination areas through the bonds of kinship, friendship, and shared community origin." These immigrant networks create ties between the host and home countries, which may also facilitate the general exchange of foreign market information as in the immigrant links hypothesis explored in this book.

Because immigrants possess knowledge of their home country markets and have home country contacts, immigrant networks can facilitate entrepreneurial trading activities between their host and home countries. This is an aspect of immigration discussed in recent case studies of immigrant entrepreneurs.[3] Although entrepreneurial activity has been found to differ between immigrant groups and destination countries, immigrants have typically found trading activities as an accessible niche to fill in the labor market (Razin 1990). In a survey of Korean immigrants in Los Angeles, Min (1990) found that the most frequent occupation of Korean immigrant entrepreneurs is importing activities (mainly trade in fashion items) with Korea. Min observed "Korean exports to the U.S. have substantially increased since the early 1970s, when a massive influx of Koreans to the U.S. started. By virtue of the advantages associated with their language and ethnic background, many Korean immigrants have been able to establish import businesses dealing in Korean-imported merchandise."

The immigrant entrepreneur literature and its case studies have observed immigrants capitalizing on their knowledge of home country language and markets to increase imports from their home country. This study proposes that these immigrant links can have effects on both imports and exports through trading activities as well as on the general increase in foreign market information available to non-immigrants.

## 2.2 IMMIGRATION AND TRADE

Interest in the relationship between immigration and trade, or more generally, factor movements and trade, can be traced back to the discussions generated by Ohlin's classic book (1933). Mundell, following Ohlin's work (1957), made use of Samuelson's factor price equalization theorem (Samuelson 1949, 1948) and showed that factor movements are substitutes to goods trade in the 2X2 Heckscher-Ohlin-Samuelson (HOS) framework. The HOS framework, in turn, has been the benchmark from which the recent literature has grown and branched off in new directions.

Starting from the HOS benchmark, later authors (Purvis, 1972; Markusen, 1983; Markusen and Svensson, 1985; and others) have argued that once some of the assumptions of the HOS model are dropped, goods trade and factor movements may be complements. In particular, relaxing any assumption that obviates factor endowments as the basis for trade will allow for the reversal of Mundell's result. For example, differences in technology between countries, non-homothetic preferences, domestic distortions in factor, or product markets can all produce complementarity between factor flows and trade. Furthermore, when one steps away from the 2X2 framework of the HOS model and allows for more than the two traditional factors of capital and labor, such as land and skilled labor, the possibility of complementarity also arises without necessarily relaxing the other assumptions of the model. Wong

(1986a) demonstrated the necessary and sufficient conditions for substitutability and complementarity to occur.

Recently, several authors have demonstrated other mechanisms by which factor flows may be complementary to trade. In particular, they have attempted to reconcile the empirical findings of others that skilled-labor-abundant countries export skilled-labor-intensive manufactured goods with the fact that these countries are also experience net in-migration of skilled labor. In a growth-theoretical context, Lucus (1988) allowed the average national level of human capital per worker to act as an externality that shifts the aggregate production function, so that workers in different countries with the same level of human capital will be paid different amounts, the worker in the human-capital-abundant country receiving the higher wage. The microeconomic foundation of this external effect of human capital is the sharing of knowledge and skills between skilled workers that occurs through both formal an informal interaction. The diffusion and growth of knowledge that takes place as a result of that interaction is modeled in Jovanovic and Rob (1989). In their model, individuals augment their knowledge through pairwise meetings at which they exchange ideas. In each time period, each individual seeking to augment his knowledge meets an agent chosen randomly from a distribution of agents. The higher the average level of human capital (knowledge) of the agents, the more "luck" agents will have with their meetings and the more rapidly knowledge will grow.

In an approach that relies on neither externalities nor differences in the cost of capital or technology, Rauch (1991) modeled managerial "talent" as an endogenous third factor generated by skilled labor. Because managers are complementary in production to skilled and unskilled labor, an increase in skilled labor generates an increase in all wages and more exports of the skilled-labor-intensive good. Leamer (1990) created a more simplified general equilibrium model of talent that also describes the observed complementarity between skilled labor migration and exports of skilled intensive goods. Rather than being an endogenous third factor, talent in Leamer's model augments the marginal productivity of workers in the capital-intensive goods industry. The more talented the workers are, the higher their wages, and the larger the wage gap between talented workers in capital- and labor-abundant countries. Consequently, the most talented have the greatest incentive to migrate to capital-abundant countries that also have a comparative advantage in the talent-using industry. Hence, the complementarity between skilled labor migration and being skilled labor abundant is explained.

Interest in the immigration of skilled workers to countries that are abundant in skilled labor is by no means a new area of interest. Bhagwati and Hamada (1974), Bhagwati and Rodriguez (1975) among others have generated a substantial body of literature on the coincident movement of labor and human capital in what has been called "the brain drain." The impetus for skilled labor emigrating from developing countries to skilled labor-abundant developed countries is usually based on a domestic distortion in the home country. Emigration causes a loss in the home country because the distortion results in the social marginal cost of emigration being larger than the private marginal cost. The first paper to consider distortions in a systematic, general equilibrium framework was by Bhagwati and Hamada (1974). It considered two distortions: an educational subsidy (which is a policy-imposed distortion) and a sticky wage (which is an endogenous distortion).

While there has been a large interest in models that describe the flow of skilled labor to skilled labor abundant countries, there has been only one author, to my knowledge, Wong (1986b) who has attempted to examine empirically the relationship between factor mobility and trade. He found a complementary relationship between immigration and overall trade. However, in his analysis he did not utilize immigration data or account for bilateral trade flow effects. He assumed that changes in the domestic labor supply have the same effects as changes in the immigrant labor supply on trade. Wong specified an indirect trade utility function and aggregate supply function and estimated, for the United States, export and income equations for three sectors: domestic goods, non-durable goods, and an aggregate imports sector. Utilizing the

Armington hypothesis (goods are differentiated between countries) Wong then calculated export and import elasticities with respect to factor mobility, assuming the skill level of immigrants is the same as natives'. He then simulated the effect on the trade balance of an increase by 1 million in the labor supply. As mentioned, a problem with this analysis is that it does not distinguish between immigrants or natives when the labor supply is augmented. Consequently, any difference in skill levels or effects of immigrant links to the home country cannot be measured.

## 2.3  IMMIGRATION, WELFARE, AND FACTOR RETURNS

In the HOS framework, welfare and factor returns are not affected by immigration because factor movements between countries affect the composition of output but not at all the returns to factors, at least when countries are diversified in production. As long as countries are not specialized in production, the marginal product curve of all factors is horizontal and immigration will not create gainers or losers. In response to this original assumption of the HOS model, several approaches have developed that analyze circumstances in which national welfare is affected and there are gainers and losers from immigration.

Of course, any analysis that includes positive externalities generated by immigration has welfare-improving consequences for the host country. This describes some of the analyses of skilled labor migration discussed above. However, in a competitive economy with no externalities, the simplest approach to analyzing immigration and welfare is the case in which some factors are fixed. Fixed factors of production generate a declining marginal product of labor in the basic HOS trade model.

With a declining marginal product for labor, the effects of immigration on the host country depend crucially on whether or not the flow of immigrants is large or small. Grubel and Scott (1966) showed that the host or home country will be neither hurt nor helped by a small increase in immigrants. Their argument may be outlined as follows. Immigration will indeed increase domestic production, but labor is paid according to its marginal product in a competitive economy with no distortions. In this economy, the loss to the host country is the wage of labor (the private marginal product of labor), which is equal to the social benefit of labor (the social marginal product of labor). Consequently, the host country neither gains nor loses as a result of immigration because the loss just offsets the gain. The same story can be applied to the country of emigration as well.

However, Berry and Soligo (1969) and Tobin (1974) showed that, in the presence of diminishing returns (declining marginal product), immigration implies a fall in wage rates and a rise in profit rates. Yet over a finite range of change, the loss to labor will not completely offset the gain to capital; there will be a gain in social surplus that represents a real domestic benefit resulting from immigration. However, there is also a real domestic loss in the country of emigration when labor leaves.

In an other approach that looks at how different subsectors of an economy are affected by immigration, Leamer (1988) showed that with regional immobility of some factors within a country, immigration can result in different earnings and output responses. For example, an increase in unskilled labor migration to the border region of a country may result in a decline in unskilled labor wages and an increase in output of the unskilled labor-intensive good in that region, but in the center region of the same country, unskilled wages may actually increase. This result depends on a third factor of production and the technology used to produce goods in the center. Leamer found indirect support for the theory by examining the regional variation in the composition of output that is explained by regional differences in the supplies of factors. Although the evidence is not conclusive, he finds that U.S. Standard Metropolitan Statistical Areas (SMSAs) with a large number of Hispanics tend to produce goods that are labor-intensive and that a substantial amount of the variation in industrial output value added across SMSAs can be accounted for by labor disaggregated by education, age, and ethnicity.

Empirical studies of the effects of immigration on domestic wages have generally not found strong evidence that immigration reduces wages of natives. In a study of U.S. immigration, Topel and LaLonde (1991) found that the effects of immigration on natives' earnings are very slight. The largest estimate they made is that a long-term doubling of immigration to an area may reduce the annual earnings of young blacks by about 4 percent. They also found that the earnings of both new and old immigrants are lower in areas where immigrants form a large or growing portion of the local labor force. However, this finding may not be because immigration lowers earnings but rather because less-skilled immigrants locate in areas where immigrants form a large share of the labor force. In examining the effect of new immigration on previous immigrant earnings (new immigrants competing the most with previous immigrants), they found that a doubling of new immigration to a locale would reduce old immigrant's earnings by less than 3 percent, but over time this effect decreases as immigrants become assimilated. For natives, this implies that new immigration has an even smaller effect on wages, given that natives are in less competition for jobs with new immigrants than are earlier immigrants.

DeFreitas (1988), using the 1980 U.S. census to investigate labor market effects of Hispanics on native groups, also found weak indications of immigration influencing native wages. Separating natives by sex, race, and ethnic origin, he found that there is no significant negative effect of Hispanic immigration on wages of any group except for black females in which the effect is small. In another study, Grossman (1982) estimated the effect of foreign-born workers on second-generation workers, and on native workers, in a sample of 19 SMSAs. In addition to the proportions of these groups in the labor force, she introduced a variable for quantity of capital. Her results implied a slight negative effect of immigration on native wages.

## 2.4 SUMMARY

The study of immigration and trade is by no means a new subject and neither is the hypothesis that immigration can be complementary to trade flows. However, until now, the study of immigration as a source of increasing trade linkages between countries has not been more than a casual speculation. The immigrant network and immigrant entrepreneur literature has provided several case studies of groups that have taken advantage of their particular knowledge of home country markets and home country contacts to engage in trading activities. The approach to immigration taken in this book is that these linkages and networks can have general effects on imports and exports as the total amount of foreign market information and trade contacts increases between the host and home countries.

# NOTES

[1] For example, see Boyd (1989).

[2] See Light et al., (1990).

[3] See, for example, Light (1985), Light and Bonacich (1988), and Razin (1990).

# Chapter 3

# General Equilibrium Model

The question addressed in this chapter is, What are the potential effects of immigrant links on the host country's welfare, factor returns, and trade? This issue is important in assessing the economic consequences of immigration as well as in understanding the political economy of immigration—that is, Who will lobby for immigration liberalizations or restrictions? Furthermore, questions concerning the changing source country distribution of immigrants can be addressed in this context. Does it make a difference to a host country's income distribution whether it receives all its immigrants from only one country or from a dozen countries? Should a host country actively promote diversity in its immigration policy, or should the country be passive?

In this chapter, a three-goods, two-factor model is developed to analyze how immigration and immigrant links affect welfare, factor returns and trade. The analysis takes the point of view of an economy that receives an inflow of foreign labor. This chapter is divided into two primary sections; the first develops a long-run model of immigrant links and trade, and the second examines the medium-run effects of immigrant links on factor returns.

In the first section, the duality approach to modeling international trade, as developed by Dixit and Norman (1980), is utilized because it can summarize, in a rather simple fashion, the supply and demand changes that result from immigration and changes in information costs due to immigrant links. The focus of this section is to examine the effects of immigrant links on trade and welfare in a simple general equilibrium model with traded and non-traded goods. Two conclusions of the model contrast against those of the standard 2X2 HOS trade model. First, although the model has only two traded goods and two factors, immigration can be a complement to trade. This result contrasts with the HOS model's implication of immigration's being solely a substitute to trade. Second, the model suggests that the total potential gains from trade will increase with immigration that decreases foreign market information costs.

In the second section, the effect of immigration and immigrant links on factor rewards is discussed. It is shown that in the medium-run with sector-specific capital and labor mobile, immigration alone tends to decrease wages, as in the specific factors model. However, with immigrant links, the tradables sector expands, thereby mitigating the downward pressure on wages. The implication that immigrant links can help prevent wages from falling may help to explain why recent empirical studies have failed to show a strong negative relationship between U.S. immigration and natives' wages.[1]

## 3.1  THE MODEL

The model under consideration consists of an open economy that produces three goods: importables ($M$), exportables ($X$), and non-tradables ($N$), with two factors labor ($L$) and capital ($K$). In this model, the rest of the world (outside the host and home countries) is so large that the migration of labor does not influence world prices of traded goods. Although there are two factors and two traded goods (which implies factor price equalization in the traditional HOS framework), the lack of foreign market information results in a wedge between the domestic and foreign prices of traded goods. Consequently, the scarce factor, which is labor in the host country, is paid more than it would be in the absence of transactions costs. All goods are produced by capital and labor, with exports being the most capital intensive and non-tradable goods the least capital intensive.

There are a large number of producers and consumers, so that perfect competition prevails, and all goods are produced with constant returns to scale. Consumers maximize utility subject to their budget constraint, and producers maximize profit subject to the available resources and technology.

The representative consumer maximizes the following utility function:

$$\max_{C_n, C_m, C_x} : U(C_n, C_m, C_x), \tag{1}$$

subject to the budget constraint:

$$C_x + pC_m + qC_n \leq Income, \tag{2}$$

where $U(\cdot)$ is the utility function, $C_n$ is the consumption of non-tradables, $C_m$ is the consumption of imports, $C_x$ is the consumption of exports, $p$ is the domestic price of importables relative to exportables inclusive of transactions costs, and $q$ is the price of non-tradables relative to exportables. Income is derived from labor wages and capital rental and is measured in terms of the exportable good.

On the production side, firms use standard technology (that is, ruling out increasing returns to scale and all increasing marginal rates of substitution and transformation) that is the same across countries to produce imports, exports, and non-tradables. Subject to standard technology, firms maximize profit

$$\max_{Q_x, Q_m, Q_n} : \Pi = (Q_x + pQ_m + qQ_n) - w_i V, \tag{3}$$

where $Q_m$ is the quantity of importables produced, $Q_n$ is the quantity of non-tradables produced, $Q_x$ is the quantity of exportables produced, $V$ is the vector of inputs, and $w_i$ is the vector of factor wages in country $i$.

The price of importables relative to exportables is equal to the international price of these goods plus the information costs involved in trading between two countries.

$$p = p^* + I(Z), \qquad (4)$$

where $p^*$ is the international price of importables relative to exportables, $I(\cdot)$ are foreign market information costs ($I(Z) \geq 0$), and $Z$ is a subset of the vector of factor inputs ($V$) and refers to those factors that can increase information about the foreign market. In this model, Z represents the stock of immigrants.

Information costs in this model are assumed to create a wedge between the domestic and international prices of imports and exports. Although the international price is not observable, it can be thought of as that price that would exist in the absence of any information costs. These costs relate to language barriers, knowledge of foreign markets structure (*i.e.*, where and how to sell products abroad) and costs associated with gaining foreign market contacts.

Assuming that foreign market information costs decrease with the flow of immigrants at a decreasing rate after some threshold in the stock of immigrants has been reached, we have if $Z \geq Z^*$: $\left[\frac{dI}{dZ} < 0,\right]$ and $\left[\frac{d^2I}{dZ^2} < 0,\right]$ where $Z^*$ is the threshold level of immigrants needed to affect information in the host country. Figure 1 describes the shape of the information cost function.

The simultaneous solutions to the producers' and consumers' maximization problems will determine the equilibrium levels of non-tradables prices, factor rewards, and outputs of all goods.

A simple way of summarizing equilibrium in the host country is to use duality theory.[2] To begin with, all other factors are assumed to be immobile across countries except labor. Furthermore, immigrants are assumed not to repatriate any income to their country of origin.

Let $E(1, p, q, u)$ stand for the expenditure function for all workers in the host country, and $R(1, p, q, V)$ the revenue function for all firms. Equations (5) through (7) summarize the model:

$$E(1, p, q, u) = R(1, p, q, V), \qquad (5)$$

$$E_q(1, p, q, u) = R_q(1, p, q, V), \qquad (6)$$

Figure 1

Information Costs and the Stock of Immigrants

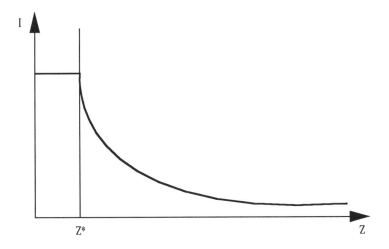

$$p = p^* + I(Z). \tag{7}$$

The partial derivative of a variable is denoted by a subscript. Thus, $R_q$ is the partial derivative of the revenue function with respect to the price of non-tradables and is the supply of non-tradables. $E_q$ is the derivative of the expenditure function with respect to the price of non-tradables, which is the Hicksian compensated demand for non-tradables. The price of exports is the numeraire.

In this one-period model, the first equation imposes external equilibrium (trade balance), the second represents internal equilibrium in the non-tradables sector, and the third is the relationship between the domestic and foreign price of importables.[3]

To determine the effects of immigration, consider the consequences of a shift in the stock of immigrants. Because the only change in the vector of factor inputs, $V$, is the inflow of immigrants, $dZ$ equals $dV$. Consequently, in what follows, the term $dV$ will substitute for $dZ$.

Totally differentiating the system gives:

$$(E_p - R_p)dp + (E_q - R_q)dq + E_u du = R_V dV, \tag{8}$$

$$(E_{qp} - R_{qp})dp + (E_{qq} - R_{qq})dq + E_{qu} du = R_{qV} dV, \tag{9}$$

$$dp = I_V dV. \tag{10}$$

Because the demand for non-tradables equals the supply of non-tradables, $(E_q - R_q) = 0$, equation (8) becomes,

$$(E_p - R_p)dp + E_u du = R_V dV. \tag{11}$$

Substituting equation (10) into equations (9) and (11) to eliminate $dp$, and noting that $\phi_n = \frac{E_{qu}}{E_u}$ is the pure income effect on the demand for non-tradables, and letting M denote imports, which are $(E_p - R_p)$, the system can be expressed as:

$$\begin{bmatrix} 0 & E_u \\ (E_{qq} - R_{qq}) & E_u \phi_n \end{bmatrix} \begin{bmatrix} dq \\ du \end{bmatrix} = \begin{bmatrix} [R_V - MI_V]dV \\ R_{qV}(E_{qp} - R_{qq})I_V dV \end{bmatrix},$$

which yields the solutions,

$$\frac{dq}{dV} = \frac{1}{\Delta}[(R_V\phi_n - R_{qV})E_u + [(E_{qp} - R_{qp}) - M\phi_n]E_uI_V], \quad (12)$$

$$\frac{du}{dV} = \frac{1}{\Delta}[-(E_{qq} - R_{qq})[R_V - MI_V]], \quad (13)$$

where $\Delta = -(E_{qq} - R_{qq})E_u$ is the determinant of the system.

Equation (12) represents the effect of immigration on the price of non-tradables, and equation (13) represents the impact of immigration on the host country's welfare defined over consumption of these three goods. These two equations are discussed in detail in the following two subsections.

### 3.1.1 The Price of Non-tradable Goods

First, note that the determinant of the system, $\Delta$, is positive because $E_u$, the change in total expenditure when utility changes, is positive. The term $-(E_{qq} - R_{qq})$ is positive because $(E_{qq})$, the own price effect on the demand for non-tradables is negative, and $(R_{qq})$, the own price effect on the supply of non-tradables is positive. That is, demand is downward sloping, and supply is upward sloping.

Equation (12) implies that changes in the price of non-tradables depend on three terms: (1) $(R_V\phi_n - R_{qV})E_u$, (2) $(E_{qp} - R_{qp})E_uI_V$, and (3) $-[M\phi_n]E_uI_V$. If immigrant links are not present (i.e., $I_V = 0$), the change in the price of non-tradables depends only on the first term.

The first term, $(R_V\phi_n - R_{qV})E_u$, represents the direct demand and supply effects of immigration on the non-tradables sector. $(R_V\phi_n)$ are the wage payments to immigrants multiplied by the pure income effect on the demand for non-tradables, and $(R_{qV})$ is the Rybczynski effect of immigration in the non-tradables sector. Wage payments will have a positive impact on the demand for non-tradable goods through the income effect, and hence will tend to increase the price of non-tradables. However, the Rybczynski effect can be either positive or negative depending on the relative capital-labor ratios in the other sectors. If the capital-labor ratio in the non-tradables sector is higher than in the importables or exportables sectors, then the Rybczynski effect is negative and the total effect of immigration on the price of non-tradables, excluding immigrant links, is positive. Otherwise, the change in the price of non-tradables is unknown because the Rybczynski effect may or may not dominate the positive income effect.

If immigrant links accompany immigration, the second and third terms are important. These respective terms relate to the substitution and income effects in the non-tradables sector when immigrant links decrease the relative price of traded goods.

The second term, $(E_{qp} - R_{qp})E_u I_V$, represents the demand and supply effects in the non-traded goods sector when the price of traded goods falls due to an increase in foreign market information. Because there are three goods in this model, any two can be complementary as long as the third is a substitute to both. If we assume that all goods are substitutes in consumption, the cross price effect on the demand for non-tradables $(E_{qp})$ is positive. On the other hand, the cross price effect on the supply of non-tradables $(R_{qp})$ must always be negative. Consequently, if all goods are substitutes in consumption, then immigrant links will induce substitution away from non-tradables and tend to decrease the price of non-tradables.

The third term, $-[M\phi_n]E_u I_V$, represents the positive income effect from decrease in the relative price of tradables on the demand for non-tradables. This increase in income will tend to put upward pressure on the demand for non-tradables, and thereby will increase the price of non-tradables.

In summary, immigrant links will cause a fall in the price of non-tradables (because of the fall in the price of traded goods) when the substitution away from non-tradables outweighs the positive income effect on the demand for non-tradables. In general, however, the overall effects of immigration and immigrant links on the price of non-tradables are uncertain.

## 3.1.2  Host Country Welfare

Equation (13) shows that the welfare effects of immigration and immigrant links depend on two factors that are both proportional to $-\frac{1}{\Delta}(E_{qq}-R_{qq})$. This expression is the determinant of the system multiplied by the own price effect on the demand and supply of non-tradables, which, as mentioned above, is positive. The first term, $(R_V)$, reflects the marginal product of labor, or the wage rate of labor, and the second term, $(-MI_V)$, reflects the increase in income due to the increase in the terms of trade as a result of new foreign market information becoming available.

The first term, $(R_V)$, is the marginal product of labor and is positive. The second term, $(-MI_V)$, represents the increase in income due to the decrease in the information costs associated with trade. This term has a positive impact on the welfare of the host country because $(I_V)$ is negative and is multiplied by another negative term,$(-M)$. Consequently, the total impact on welfare from immigration and immigrant links will be positive, assuming, of course, there are no factor market distortions.

Summarizing the effects of labor migration on the price of non-tradables and welfare, the following can be said: (1) If the new demand for non-tradables equals the change in the supply of non-tradables and substitution effect outweighs the income effect, then the price of non-tradables will fall. Otherwise, the change in the price of non-tradables is uncertain. (2) Welfare will increase in the host country as long as immigrant links decrease trade information costs. Although the home country is not the focus of this analysis, it is rather straightforward to demonstrate that welfare in the home country will also increase if emigration from the home country results in a decrease in foreign market information costs.

## *3.1.3  Trade*

This section examines the effects of immigration and immigrant links on trade flows. To determine what these effects are, the expression for imports, $M = (E_p - R_p)$, is differentiated with respect to a change in immigration. Because this model does not include a capital account, this expression also represents movements in exports. So, a relative price change that directly affects imports is also a price change that directly affects exports.

The change in imports due to immigration is:

$$\frac{dM}{dV} = -R_{pV} + (E_{pp} - R_{pp})I_V + [E_{pq} - R_{qp}]\frac{dq}{dV} + \phi_n E_u \frac{du}{dV}. \quad (14)$$

The first term represents the direct effect of immigration on the change in supply of importables. The second term is the own price effect on demand for and supply of importables due to a change in information. The third term represents the substitution into or out of imports when the price of non-tradables changes. The last term is the effect of a change in welfare (the income effect) in the importables sector.

The first term, the direct effect on imports $(-R_{pV})$, can be positive, or negative depending on the sign of the Rybczynski effect. Maintaining the assumption that the import-competing sector is relatively labor intensive compared with the exports sector, the Rybczynski effect will be positive and, hence, the sign of the first term will be negative. Under this condition, when there is an increase in the labor supply, labor flows into the import-competing sector, which results in an increase in the production of import competing goods and a decrease in imports.

The second term, $(E_{pp} - R_{pp})I_V$, represents the own price effect on the demand and supply of importables. With a decrease in information costs, the price of imports goes down so the consumption of imports will increase, while host country production falls. The net effect of this term results in an increase in imports.

The third term, $[E_{pq} - R_{qp}]\frac{dq}{dV}$, relates to the cross substitution effects between importables and non-tradables. If all goods are substitutes in consumption, an increase in the price of non-tradables will tend to increase imports.

The fourth term, $\phi_n E_u \frac{du}{dV}$, shows how a change in welfare will affect imports. This is essentially the income effect and is positive when immigrant links decrease the information costs associated with trade.

In general, the direction of the change in imports is ambiguous because the values of the first and third terms, the effect on production and the substitution effect from a change in the price of non-tradables, are indeterminate. The second and fourth terms, the own price effect and income effect, are positive and will always tend to increase imports.

Although the change in trade is ambiguous in the model, the following can be said: If a marginal increase in the flow of immigrants brings a large enough decrease in the transactions costs to trade, imports (and exports) will increase. This suggests that immigrants who transmit a relatively large amount of information about their home country will have a positive effect on bilateral trade.

# 3.2 IMMIGRATION AND FACTOR REWARDS

This section takes a detailed look at the medium-run implications of immigrant linkson changes in factor rewards and output mix. Under the assumptions made above, exports are the most capital intensive, and non-tradables are the least capital intensive. The capital intensity of imports lies between exports and non-tradables. Because this is a medium-run analysis, capital is assumed to be sector specific, but labor is mobile between sectors.[4]

The initial labor market equilibrium is depicted in Figure 2. The horizontal axis represents the total amount of labor available to the host economy and the vertical axis represents the wage in terms of importables.[5] The demand for labor in the tradables goods sector is the curve labeled $L_T$, and is equal to the horizontal sum of the demand for labor in the importables sector $L_I$ and that in the exportables sector. The demand for labor by the non-tradables goods sector is shown by the curve $L_N$. The initial equilibrium is characterized by a wage rate equal to $W_0$, with $O_T L_A$ labor used in producing importables, $L_A L_B$ used in producing exportables, and $O_N L_B$ labor used in producing non-tradables.

With an increase in immigration, the supply of labor to all sectors increases which, is represented by the horizontal axis expanding by the distance $O_N O_{N'}$. If the price of non-tradables does not change and immigrant links are absent, then the wage rate will

Figure 2

Labor Market Equilibrium with Immigration and No Immigrant
Links

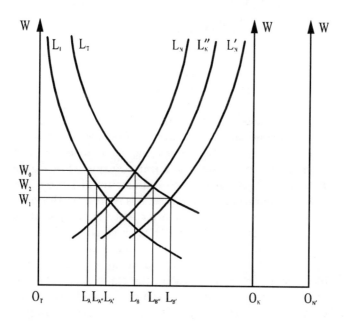

fall from $W_0$ to $W_1$. If the price of non-tradables does increase, the labor demand curve for non-tradables will shift out to $L_N''$, causing wages to rise from $W_1$ to $W_2$. Consequently, the existence of non-tradable goods may decrease the pressure for wages to fall. A possible but unlikely case is if the price of non-tradables increases to such a degree that wages actually rise above the initial equilibrium. This is possible if non-tradables, as a whole, are necessities and immigrants spend a large proportion of their income on these goods.

Figure 3 shows the final equilibrium depicted in Figure 2 with the added labor market adjustment due to immigrant links. The accompanying reduction in transactions costs will result in a higher price received for exports and will generate an upward shift in the $L_T$ curve to $L_T'$. The new curve will intersect the $L_N''$ curve at $A$, but this is not the final equilibrium. Whereas the domestic price of exports relative to imports rises from the decrease in information costs, the relative price of non-tradables, as discussed above, can either increase or decrease depending on the income and substitution effects.

Assuming the income effect does not outweigh the substitution effect, the price of non-tradables will fall because of immigrant links. As a result, $L_N''$ will shift downward (by less than the increase in $L_T$) to $L_N'''$ and the final equilibrium will be achieved at $B$ with the wage rate at $W_3$. The production of non-tradables falls and results in a decrease in labor demand in that sector from $O_{N'}L_{B''}$ to $O_{N'}L_{B'''}$. The production of importables goes down and causes labor in that sector to leave, which is shown by a shift from $O_T L_{A''}$ to $O_T L_{A'''}$. As drawn in the diagram, labor moves out of the non-tradables and import-competing sectors and into the exports sector as the production of non-tradables and importables goes down. Consequently, because of immigrant links, the exports sector increases production and the wage rate rises above a level that would result in the absence of immigrant link effects.

Table 4 summarizes changes in the wage rate and the return to capital due to immigration and immigrant links that decrease transactions costs. $K_E$ represents capital in the exports

Figure 3

Labor Market Equilibrium with Immigration and Immigrant Links

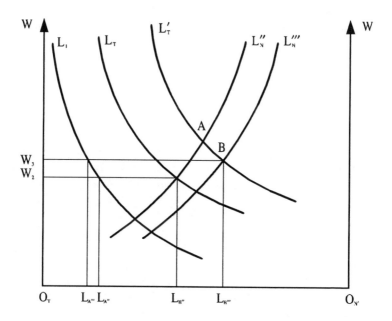

sector, $K_I$ represents capital in the imports sector, and $K_N$ represents capital in the non-traded goods sector. With immigration absent immigrant links, labor loses in terms of all goods. Capital, on the other hand, gains in terms of exports and imports, while it can either gain or lose in terms of non-tradables, depending on the magnitude of the price change in the non-tradables sector.

Table 4

Change in Factor Rewards With Immigration

| Factor Rewards in Terms of | With an increase in immigration | | | | Change due to Immigrant Links | | | |
|:---:|:---:|:---:|:---:|:---:|:---:|:---:|:---:|:---:|
| | $L$ | $K_E$ | $K_I$ | $K_N$ | $L$ | $K_E$ | $K_I$ | $K_N$ |
| Exports | − | + | + | + | ? | + | − | − |
| Imports | − | + | + | + | + | + | − | − |
| Non-tradables | − | ? | ? | ? | + | + | ? | − |

If immigration is accompanied by immigrant links, labor will gain in terms of importables and non-tradables, while it may gain or lose in terms of exportables. As drawn in Figure 3, labor loses in terms of exportables because wages have increased less than the price of exportables. Capital in the importables sector loses in terms of all goods except in terms of non-tradables, where it may gain or lose. Capital in the export sector gains in terms of all goods, while capital in the non-tradables sector loses in terms of all goods.

The important point to be stressed here is that unlike the traditional specific factors model, this model demonstrates that the larger immigrant links are, the less labor will lose as a result of immigration. This is due to the trade-enhancing effects of immigrant links. To some degree, this may help explain why a number of empirical studies have found the effect of immigration on natives' wages to be slight.

# 3.3  SUMMARY

This chapter investigates an aspect of immigration that until now has received little attention—namely, the foreign market information that immigrants generate. This new information in the host country can decrease the transactions costs of trade by making it easier to obtain knowledge of the immigrant's home-country language, market structure, and foreign contacts.

The model developed in this chapter explains how immigration and immigrant links to the home country can affect welfare, trade and factor returns. The effects of immigration are examined in terms of both tradable and non-tradable goods. Two conclusions derived from the model contrast sharply with those of the standard 2X2 HOS model. First, although the model has only two traded goods and two factors, immigration can be a complement to trade, which contrasts with the HOS implication of immigration's being a substitute to trade. Second, by increasing the available amount of foreign market information in the host country, immigration increases welfare.

The effects of immigrant links on factor rewards have also been discussed. It was shown that, in the medium-run with capital-sector specific and labor mobile, immigration alone tends to decrease wages, as is the case in the specific factors model. However, with immigrant links, the tradables sector expands and tends to mitigate the downward pressure on labor wages.

Several interesting facets of the relationship between immigration and immigrant links remain to be explored. A particularly useful research project would be to examine the differences in the domestic wage response to increases in immigration from different immigrant source countries, addressing the question of whether increases in the size of immigrant communities with the largest immigrant-link effects have the smallest effects on natives' wages. The results would provide useful information on the ability of the

United States to increase immigration without placing a large burden on the natives who compete the most with immigrants.

# NOTES

[1] See, for example, Topel and LaLonde (1990) and Borjas (1990).

[2] See Dixit and Norman (1980) pages 146-149, S. Edwards (1987).

[3] Since there is only one period in this model, external equilibrium will always exist and because there is no capital account in this model, external equilibrium implies trade balance.

[4] In the short-run, both labor and capital would be sector specific.

[5] This diagram is an adaptation for the three good case of the Ricardo-Viner models of Jones (1971), Mayer (1974), and Mussa (1974). See S. Edwards (1988).

# Chapter 4

# Analytical Model

In the previous chapter, the effects of immigration and immigrant links were examined in a general equilibrium model with tradable and non-tradable goods. Although many implications of the model were dependent on the relative strengths of supply and demand shifts, it was shown that the larger the decrease in transactions costs from immigrant links, the greater is trade between the host and home countries. The purpose of this chapter is not to develop an alternative model of immigration, but rather to provide an empirically tractable, reduced form model for the empirical analysis that follows.

Unlike the general equilibrium model introduced earlier, the focus here will be exclusively on the tradables sector. The implicit assumption is that any adjustment in the non-tradables sector is small and can be separated from the equilibrium in the rest of the economy. Therefore, we can take equilibrium in the non-tradables sector as exogenous to equilibrium in the tradables sector.

The model developed is a modification of Bergstrand's (1985) microeconomic foundation of the gravity equation.[1] The essential feature developed here is the introduction of endogenous transactions costs that decline with the introduction of foreign market information supplied by immigrants. The model consists of $N$ countries, each of which produces goods that are differentiated according to the country of destination. Production takes place using a given endowment of labor from a country's own native population and an immigrant population that comes from a subset of the other $(N-1)$ countries. Producers maximize profits subject to constant elasticity of transformation (CET) technology, and consumers maximize a constant elasticity of substitution (CES) utility function subject to a budget constraint.

## 4.1 SUPPLY

Assuming identical technologies across countries, labor is allocated across industries for every country $i$ according to CET joint production surface.[2] In this production surface, labor in country $i$ can be transformed into producing different foreign goods at a constant elasticity, but it cannot be transformed from producing foreign goods to domestic goods at the same constant elasticity.

$$L_i = \left\{ \left[ \left( \sum_{k=1}^{N} X_{ik}^{\phi} \right)^{1/\phi} \right]^{\delta} + X_{ii}^{\delta} \right\}^{1/\delta}, \qquad (15)$$

$$i = 1, \ldots, N \text{ and } k \neq i,$$

where

| | |
|---|---|
| $L_i$ | is defined as a single factor of production available to country $i$ (that is, domestic labor and immigrant labor), |
| $X_{ik}$ | is country $i$'s good supplied to country $k$, |
| $X_{ii}$ | is country $i$'s good supplied to the domestic market, |
| $\delta = (\eta + 1)/\eta,$ | where $\eta$ is the elasticity of transformation between any two goods in country $i$ $(0 \leq \eta \leq \infty)$, and |
| $\phi = (\gamma + 1)/\gamma,$ | where $\gamma$ is the CET among exportable goods $(0 \leq \gamma \leq \infty)$. |

Maximizing profit subject to the CET technology gives $N^2$ first-order conditions and generates $N(N-1)$ bilateral exports supply equations

$$X_{ij}^S = Y_i P_{ij}^{*\,\gamma} \left[\left(\Sigma' P_{ik}^{*\,1+\gamma}\right)^{1/(1+\gamma)}\right]^{-(\gamma-\eta)}$$
$$\times \left[\left[\left(\Sigma' P_{ik}^{*\,1+\gamma}\right)^{1/(1+\gamma)}\right]^{1+\eta} + P_{ii}^{*\,1+\eta}\right]^{-1}, \quad (16)$$

where
$P_{ik}^* = P_{ik}/(T_{ik}C_{ik}Z_{ik})$     is the price received for selling $i$'s product in the $k^{th}$ country,

$P_{ik}$     is the price of $i$'s product sold in the $k^{th}$ market,

$T_{ik}$     is 1 plus the ad valorem tariff rate on $i$'s product sold in the $k^{th}$ market,

$C_{ik}$     is a transport cost factor assumed to be a function of distance ($C_{ik} \geq 1$),

$Z_{ik}$     are the costs associated with gaining foreign market information about country $k$ in country $i$ ($Z_{ik} \geq 1$),

$Y_i$     is total income paid to labor ($Y_i = W_i L_i$), where $W_i$ is the wage, and

$\Sigma'$     denotes summation over $k = 1, \ldots, N, k \neq i$.

The equation above shows that country $i$'s supply of its differentiated product to the foreign markets depends on its income ($Y_i$), the price of that product in country $j$ ($P_{ij}$) and in the domestic market $(P_{ii})$, and the price of the product in the other foreign markets $(\Sigma' P_{ik}^*)$.

The transactions costs to trade $(Z_{ik})$ are assumed to be a function of the foreign market information carried by immigrants. That is, $Z_{ik} = f(M_{ik})$, where $M_{ik}$ is the number of immigrants from country $k$ in country $i$; $f(\cdot)$ represents the transactions costs related to language, knowledge of foreign markets, and the lack of access to foreign contacts. These costs are assumed to be a decreasing function of the foreign market information carried by immigrants: $\frac{dZ_{ik}}{dM_{ik}} < 0$.

With complete information across countries and no transportation costs or tariffs, the price of a traded good produced for the domestic market is the same as its price in the foreign market. With incomplete information about foreign countries, producers of tradable goods find that the actual price they receive for these goods abroad is less than the home price—the difference being transactions costs.

Given the assumptions about the role of immigrants discussed above and assuming that information about the foreign market increases with the flow of immigrants at a decreasing rate, we have $\frac{d^2 Z_{ik}}{dM_{ik}^2} > 0$.

To simplify the following presentation, the functional form of transactions costs that satisfies these conditions is presented with the empirical model in the next chapter.

## 4.2  DEMAND

Consumers in all countries are assumed to share the following CES utility function:[3]

$$U_j = \left\{ \left[ \left( \sum_{k=1}^{N} X_{kj}^{\theta} \right)^{1/\theta} \right]^{\psi} + X_{jj}^{\psi} \right\}^{1/\psi}, \qquad (17)$$

$$j = 1, \ldots, N \text{ and } k \neq j,[4]$$

where

$X_{kj}$     is the country $k$'s good demanded by country $j$;

$X_{jj}$     is the good that is produced and demanded domestically;

$\psi = (\mu - 1)/\mu,$     where $\mu$ is the CES between domestic goods and imported goods in the host country $(0 \leq \mu \leq \infty)$; and

$\theta = (\sigma - 1)/\sigma,$     where $\sigma$ is the CES among importable goods $(0 \leq \sigma \leq \infty)$.

Maximizing utility subject to income $(Y_j)$ yields $N+1$ first-order conditions and $N(N-1)$ bilateral aggregate import demand equations

$$X_{ij}^D = Y_j P_{ij}^{-\sigma} \left[ \left( \Sigma'' P_{kj}^{1-\sigma} \right)^{1/(1-\sigma)} \right]^{\sigma - \mu}$$

$$\times \left\{ \left[ \left( \Sigma'' P_{kj}^{1-\sigma} \right)^{1/(1-\sigma)} \right]^{1-\mu} + P_{jj}^{1-\mu} \right\}^{-1}, \quad (18)$$

where $\sum''$ denotes summation over $k = 1, \ldots, N, k \neq j$. Equation (18) shows that country $j$'s demand for country $i$'s product $(X_{ij})$ depends on its income $(Y_j)$, the price of country $i$'s product $(P_{ij})$ and its own domestic product $(P_{jj})$, and the price of other foreign products available $(\Sigma'' P_{kj})$.

## 4.3 EQUILIBRIUM

Solving the complete system of supply and demand equations for $N^2$ equilibrium conditions,

$$X_{ij} = X_{ij}^D = X_{ij}^S, \quad (19)$$

yields $2N^2$ solutions for quantities and prices and N solutions for country incomes as functions of the exogenous variables $T_{ij}$, $C_{ij}$,

$Z_{ij}$, and $L_i$. However, the system can be simplified by assuming that for each country individual bilateral trade flows are small relative to total trade, so individual bilateral prices can be taken as given. The small-market assumption implies that changes in $X_{ij}$ and $P_{ij}$ that equilibrate demand and supply for traded goods between two countries have a negligible impact on incomes and prices in other markets. Consequently, combining equation (16) with equations (18) and (19) yields solutions for bilateral prices as well as trade flows, and multiplying these solutions together yields the value of aggregate trade flows:

$$
\begin{aligned}
P_{ij}X_{ij} = \; & Y_i^{(\sigma-1)/(\gamma+\sigma)} Y_j^{(\gamma+1)/(\gamma+\sigma)} C_{ij}^{-\sigma(\gamma+1)/(\gamma+\sigma)} \\
& \times T_{ij}^{-\sigma(\gamma+1)/(\gamma+\sigma)} Z_{ij}^{-\sigma(\gamma+1)/(\gamma+\sigma)} \\
& \times \left( \Sigma' P_{ik}^{*\,1+\gamma} \right)^{-(\sigma-1)(\gamma-\eta)/(1+\gamma)(\gamma+\sigma)} \\
& \times \left( \Sigma'' P_{kj}^{1-\sigma} \right)^{(\gamma+1)(\sigma-\mu)/(1-\sigma)(\gamma+\sigma)} \\
& \times \left[ \left( \Sigma' P_{ik}^{*\,1+\gamma} \right)^{(1+\eta)/(1+\gamma)} + P_{ii}^{1+\eta} \right]^{-(\sigma-1)/(\gamma+\sigma)} \\
& \times \left[ \left( \Sigma'' P_{kj}^{1-\sigma} \right)^{(1-\mu)/(1-\sigma)} + P_{jj}^{1-\mu} \right]^{-(\gamma+1)/(\gamma+\sigma)} \quad (20)
\end{aligned}
$$

where $P_{ij}X_{ij}$ is the value of aggregate trade flows from country $i$ to country $j$.

The small-market assumption yields a reduced-form bilateral trade equation with $Y_i$ and $Y_j$ treated exogenously, as well as foreign prices (other than those specifically between countries $i$ and $j$) and domestic prices.

The value of aggregate trade flows from country $i$ to country $j$ depends on nine terms. In the order of their appearance in the equation, they are (1) the income of the exporting country, (2) the income of the importing country, (3) transportation costs, (4) tariffs, (5) transactions costs associated with lack of foreign market information, (6) an export price index for exports to all other countries to which the exporting country exports, (7) an import price index for imports from all other countries from which the importing country imports, (8) an index of domestic prices for the exporting country, and (9) an index of domestic prices for the importing country.

These nine terms are of three types: income terms reflecting potential demand and supply; wedges between the export and import price of traded goods due to transportation costs, tariffs, and lack of foreign market information; and price terms reflecting substitution effects.

Only four terms in equation (20) can be signed *a priori*. These terms are the income in the importing country $(Y_j)$, which has a positive effect on trade, and the wedges between the export price and import price of the traded goods $(C_{ij}, T_{ij}, \text{ and } Z_{ij})$, which negatively affect the volume of bilateral trade.

The effect of the other terms on bilateral trade flows will depend on the relative magnitudes of the supply and demand elasticities. For example, if the demand elasticity of substitution among imports $(\sigma)$ exceeds 1, the exporting country's income and overall price index will have, respectively, positive effects and negative effects on trade flows. Additionally, if the supply elasticity of transformation among exports $(\gamma)$ exceeds the overall supply elasticity between exports and domestic goods $(\eta)$, the exporting country's export price index will have a negative effect on trade. The importing country's import price index will have a positive effect on trade if the demand elasticity of substitution among imports exceeds the overall elasticity between domestic and imported products $(\mu)$. Finally, the importing country's overall price index will have a negative or positive effect on trade depending on whether $\mu$ is less than or greater than 1.

With a few modifications, equation (20) will serve as the basis for the empirical analysis of the effects of immigrant information on bilateral trade flows.

# 4.4  SUMMARY

In this chapter, an empirically tractable bilateral trade model of immigrant links was developed. In this model goods are differentiated by country of origin and consumers' utility depends on the variety of goods available. By supplying foreign market information, immigrants decease the transactions costs to trade between the immigrant's host and home countries. This fall in transactions costs, in turn, results in a decrease in the wedge between the foreign and domestic price of traded goods and increases bilateral trade flows. With a few modifications, the model developed here will be used to analyze the effects of immigrant links on U.S. bilateral trade flows.

# NOTES

[1] The gravity equation has been used in a variety of international trade applications because it provides an empirically tractable framework. For other theoretical foundations of the gravity equation, see Anderson (1979) and Helpman and Krugman (1985).

[2] See Bergstrand (1985) and Powell and Gruen (1968).

[3] This is a form of the Dixit-Stiglitz (1977) utility function in which utility is derived from the variety and quantity of goods available.

[4] Note that the subscript $j$ is used on utility, while the $i$ subscript is used for the profit function. The demanders of goods are denoted with the $j$ subscript, while suppliers are denoted with the $i$ subscript.

# Chapter 5

# Empirical Results

The question addressed in this chapter is, Do immigrant links to the home country enhance bilateral trade flows between the home and host countries? As mentioned earlier, recent case studies of immigrant networks and immigrant entrepreneurs suggest evidence of immigrant links, but no comprehensive study of these effects has yet been undertaken. This chapter probes the empirical relevance of immigrant links in facilitating trade between the United States and the home countries of its immigrant population.

Building on the model from the previous chapter, the analysis explores immigrant links to the home country utilizing a panel data set of 47 U.S. trading partners. Sixteen years of data on the types of products imported and exported, the size and source country distribution of the immigrant stocks, and immigrant characteristics are used in the analysis. As a preview of the results, the analysis reveals that immigrant links to the home country have a strong positive impact on exports and imports, with the greatest effects on consumer manufactured exports. These effects tend to increase at a decreasing rate as the size of the immigrant community grows, and they also depend crucially on the types of goods traded.

# 5.1 DISTINGUISHING ALTERNATIVE HYPOTHESES

Ideally, the most direct way to examine immigrant links would be to measure immigration and foreign market information and then observe directly their relationship with bilateral trade flows. Unfortunately, there are no observable data on the foreign market information carried by immigrants or the transactions costs to trade. However, with available country-specific data on immigration, immigrant characteristics, and bilateral trade flows, immigrant-link effects may be inferred by analyzing the relationship among these variables. A positive relationship between immigration from a particular country and bilateral trade flows with the same country may suggest that immigrant links to the home country do exist. Whether a positive relationship between immigration and bilateral trade flows can be attributed solely to immigrant links is an important question and depends on other feasible alternative hypotheses that are consistent with the data. In the following paragraphs, I discuss some of these alternative hypotheses and ways of empirically distinguishing the immigrant-link hypothesis.

The traditional factor endowment model of trade can be consistent with the observation of trade flows being complementary to immigration if labor is the host country's abundant factor.[1] Furthermore, models that include human capital externalities or industry-specific economies of scale are also consistent with complementarity between immigration and trade flows.[2] However, none of these models make predictions for the relationship between immigration and bilateral trade flows after controlling for cross-country differences in endowments. Thus, if immigration is found to be complementary to bilateral trade flows, controlling for differences in factor endowments between countries, then this observation would suggest that a mechanism other than those mentioned above is at least partially responsible for determining bilateral trade flows.

Another alternative hypothesis is that immigrants have a greater preference for home country products, which leads to a direct increase in imports of home country products because of increased consumption. Because both this hypothesis and the immigrant-link hypothesis can imply an increase in bilateral trade flows with immigration, it becomes slightly more difficult to distinguish between them. However, an observational difference between these two hypotheses is that the immigrant preference hypothesis implies an increase in imports, whereas the immigrant-link hypothesis implies a direct increase in exports as well as imports.[3] As a result, if only imports of home country consumer goods are influenced by immigration, then probably the relevant hypothesis is immigrant preference for home country products. On the other hand, if only consumer or producer exports are influenced by immigration, then probably the immigrant-link hypothesis is the most relevant one. A combination of effects on all exports and imports would indicate that both hypotheses may be important.

The empirical investigation that follows will try to distinguish between these hypotheses by examining the relationship between immigration and bilateral trade flows for both exports and imports and for consumer, producer, and aggregate trade flows. This analysis begins with the development of the empirical model and is followed by the empirical estimation of the model.

## 5.2  EMPIRICAL MODEL

Because the primary focus of this empirical analysis is to examine immigrant-link effects on U.S. bilateral trade flows both over time and across countries, the analysis uses time-series as well as cross-sectional information. Given that desired trade flows (equation (19) in the previous chapter) may depart from actual flows over time because of decision, production, or delivery lags, the empirical analysis will approximate these possible dynamic effects by a simple flow-adjustment specification. The flow adjustment is incorporated into the log transformed empirical model by including a lagged value of logged trade flows as an explanatory variable.

The hypothesis that immigrants provide foreign market

information that decreases the transactions costs to trade at a decreasing rate is represented by the following functional form of the stock of immigrants from country $j$ in the United States:

$$Z_{us,j} = A e^{-\rho[M_{us,j}/(\vartheta + M_{us,j})]},$$
$$\rho > 0, \vartheta > 0, A > 0,$$

where $Z_{us,j}$ represents the transactions costs to trade associated with obtaining foreign market information about country $j$ in the United States. This functional form captures the assumptions that the foreign market information brought by immigrants decreases the transactions costs to trade at a decreasing rate. The parameter $\rho$ determines the size of the immigrant information effects on transactions costs, and $A$ is simply a constant. The parameter $\vartheta$ determines the curvature of this function, or the sensitivity of transactions costs to the size of the immigrant stock. When substituting this functional form for transactions costs back into the reduced-form trade flow (equation 20), the overall effect of immigration on trade is positive. In the trade equation, the exponent on the immigrant information variable, $[M_{us,j}/(\vartheta + M_{us,j})]$, is

$$\tilde{\beta} = \rho \times \sigma(\gamma + 1)/(\gamma + \sigma) > 0.$$

Because $\vartheta$ determines the curvature of the transactions costs function, its value can tell us something about the size of the stock of immigrants at which most of the marginal benefit to an additional immigrant is exhausted. For example, in the estimated trade equation, 90 percent of the immigrant information effects will be exhausted when $e^{\tilde{\beta}[M_{us,j}/(\vartheta + M_{us,j})]} = [.90 \times (e^{\tilde{\beta}} - 1) + 1]$, where $e^{\tilde{\beta}}$ is the maximum value of information effects and 1 is the minimum value.[4] Taking logarithms of this function and solving for $M_{us,j}$ in terms of $\vartheta$, we find $M_{us,j} = \vartheta \times [\log(\cdot)/\tilde{\beta}]/\{1 - (\log(\cdot)/\tilde{\beta})\}$, where $\log(\cdot) = \log[.90 \times (e^{\tilde{\beta}} - 1) + 1]$. Consequently, this shows the relationship between the size of the immigrant stock $(M_{us,j})$ and the sensitivity parameter $(\vartheta)$ when 90 percent of the benefits to the foreign market information are realized.

The effects of the skill level and the length of stay of immigrants are addressed by including measures of the ratio of skilled immigrants to unskilled immigrants and the average length of stay of the immigrant stock. To account for possible non-linearities in the effects of length of stay, the length-of-stay variable and its squared value are both included in the regression equations. It is possible that as the length of stay increases, the ability of immigrants to incorporate their foreign market information into the United States increases. However, the rate of this increase may diminish if immigrant foreign market information becomes obsolete over time.

In accordance with the theoretical model, bilateral trade flows from country $i$ to country $j$ are described as a function of income in the two countries, tariffs, transportation costs, information costs that decrease with the increasing number of immigrants, and a set of price terms that represents a type of price index of import and export prices. Because country-specific data for the price terms are not available, proxies are used. $\left(\Sigma' P_{ik}^{1+\gamma}\right)$, which is an index of all of country $i$'s export prices except the export prices of goods going to country $j$, is proxied by country $i$'s export unit value index, and $\left(\Sigma'' P_{kj}^{*\,1-\sigma}\right)$, which is an index of all of country $j$'s import prices except the import prices of goods coming from country $i$, is proxied by country $j$'s import unit value index.[5] Similarly, $\left[\left(\Sigma' P_{ik}^{1+\gamma}\right)^{(1+\eta)/(1+\gamma)} + P_{ii}^{1+\eta}\right]$, which is an index of all of country $i$'s prices, is proxied by country $i$'s gross domestic product (GDP) deflator, and $\left[\left(\Sigma'' P_{kj}^{*\,1-\sigma}\right)^{(1-\mu)/(1-\sigma)} + P_{jj}^{1-\mu}\right]$, which is an index of all of country $j$'s prices, is proxied by country $j$'s GDP deflator.[6]

Besides differences in tariff rates and transportation costs that were explicitly modeled, there are many country-specific institutional, language, distance, and factor endowment differences that may influence bilateral trade flows. Because many of these country-specific effects do not change over time (for example, language and distance) they cannot all be included jointly in the pooled cross-sectional time series analysis due to prefect multicollinearity. Consequently, to account for these factors, only country-specific dummy variables are included in the estimating equations.[7]

Differences in market size between the United States and its trading partners are controlled for by including the population of the United States and its trading partners multiplicatively in the estimating equations.

Given these preliminaries, the estimated equations describing export flows from the United States to its trading partners take the nonlinear form

$$
\begin{aligned}
\log EX_{us,j} = \; & \alpha_0 \log EX_{t-1} + \alpha_1 \log Y_{us} + \alpha_2 \log Y_j \\
& + \alpha_3 \log POP_{us} + \alpha_4 \log POP_j \\
& + \alpha_5 \log P_{us} + \alpha_6 \log P_j + \alpha_7 \log Px_{us} \\
& + \alpha_8 \log Pi_j + \alpha_9 (M_{us,j}/(\alpha_{10} + M_{us,j})) \\
& + \alpha_{11}(SKUK) + \alpha_{12}(STAY) + \alpha_{13}(STAY^2) \\
& + \alpha_{14}(D_1) + \ldots + \alpha_n(D_n)) + \varepsilon,
\end{aligned}
\tag{21}
$$

and the estimated import equations take the form

$$
\begin{aligned}
\log IM_{j,us} = \; & \beta_0 \log IM_{t-1} + \beta_1 \log Y_{us} + \beta_2 \log Y_j \\
& + \beta_3 \log POP_{us} + \beta_4 \log POP_j \\
& + \beta_5 \log P_{us} + \beta_6 \log P_j + \beta_7 \log Px_j \\
& + \beta_8 \log Pi_{us} + \beta_9 (M_{us,j}/(\beta_{10} + M_{us,j}) \\
& + \beta_{11}(SKUK) + \beta_{12}(STAY) + \beta_{13}(STAY^2) \\
& + \beta_{14}(D_1) + \ldots + \beta_n(D_n) + \upsilon,
\end{aligned}
\tag{22}
$$

where

| | |
|---|---|
| $EX_{us,j}$ | is exports of goods from the United States to the home country $j$, |
| $IM_{j,us}$ | is imports of goods from the home country $j$ to the United States, |
| $IM_{t-1}$ and $EX_{t-1}$ | are dependent variables lagged one year, |
| $\alpha$ and $\beta$ | are the estimated parameters ($\alpha_{10}$ and $\beta_{10}$ correspond to the immigrant information sensitivity parameters), |
| $Y_{us}$ and $Y_j$ | are the U.S. and home-country GDPs, |
| $POP_{us}$ and $POP_j$ | are the U.S. and home-country populations, |
| $P_{us}$ and $P_j$ | are the U.S. and home-country GDP deflators, |
| $Px_{us}$ and $Px_j$ | are the U.S. and home-country export unit value indexes, |
| $Pi_{us}$ and $Pi_j$ | are the U.S. and home-country import unit value indexes, |
| $M_{us,j}$ | is the number of immigrants from home country $j$ in the United States, |
| $SKUK_{us,j}$ | is the ratio of skilled immigrants to unskilled immigrants from home country $j$ in the United States, |
| $STAY_{us,j}$ | is the average length of stay of the immigrants in the United States, |
| $D_j$ | is the dummy variable for the home country $j$, and |
| $\varepsilon$ and $\upsilon$ | are i.i.d. error terms and corr$(\varepsilon, \upsilon) = 0$. |

Notice that the lagged dependent variable is included in the estimating equations to account for possible decision, production, and delivery lags. The primary difference between the explanatory variables of equations (21) and (22) is the included price variables. In the export equation, U.S. export unit values and country $j$'s unit import values are included; in the import equation, U.S. import unit values and country $j$'s export unit values are included.

This specification is implied by equation (20). Another variable suggested by the analytical model but not included in the estimating equations here is the number of immigrants from the United States in the home countries. These data are unavailable.[8]

As mentioned earlier, only two coefficients can be signed *a priori*: (1) the positive effect of the importing country's income on bilateral trade flows (in the export equations, this is country $j$'s income, $\alpha_2 > 0$, and in the import equations, this is U.S. income, $\beta_1 > 0$) and (2) the positive effect of the size of the immigrant stock on bilateral trade through the decrease in transactions costs, $\alpha_9 > 0$ and $\beta_9 > 0$.

Although the effects of immigrant characteristics on foreign market information are not explicitly modeled, it is plausible to expect that as the ratio of skilled immigrants to unskilled immigrants rises, information about the home country will increase ($\alpha_{11}$ and $\beta_{11} > 0$), and as the length of stay of immigrants increases, information increases ($\alpha_{12}$ and $\beta_{12} > 0$), but at a decreasing rate ($\alpha_{13}$ and $\beta_{13} < 0$). Home country and U.S. populations are not signed *a priori* because market size can have a negative effect on trade if economies of scale are present or a positive effect if a larger population allows for more specialization through a greater division of labor. The effects of the remaining variables are, *a priori*, ambiguous and are determined by relative magnitudes of the supply and demand elasticities.

The next section takes a preliminary look at the data in preparation for estimating equations (21) and (22).

# 5.3 PRELIMINARY DATA ANALYSIS

The purpose of this section is to show the inferences that can be drawn from the data in a simple bivariate framework. Because the data set has been constructed to investigate the relationship between immigration and bilateral trade flows, that is the primary focus here.[9] A positive relationship between the immigrant stock and bilateral trade flows is suggestive of the immigrant link hypothesis. Summary statistics are used to illustrate the movements in the immigrant stock and trade flows for the partner countries of the United States. Some tentative conclusions are drawn.

Tables 5, 6, and 7 show correlations between immigrant stock, lagged immigrant stock and bilateral trade flows for the United States. The first table, Table 5 shows the simple correlation between home country $i$'s immigrant stock in the United States and bilateral trade flows of country $i$ with the United States without controlling for any country-specific aspects. Table 6 shows the degree of correlation between the share of home country $i$'s immigrants in the total immigrant stock of the United States and the share of bilateral trade with home country $i$ in total trade of the United States. Table 7 is similar to Table 6 but gives a bit better indication of the relationship between immigration and bilateral trade flows by controlling for the size of the home and the host countries' world trade. It shows the correlation between bilateral trade with home country $i$ relative to the total trade flows of the host and home country and the share home country $i$'s immigrants in the total immigrant stock of the United States.

The data include the entire, pooled cross-section time-series sample for 47 U.S. trading partners over 16 years between 1970 and 1986. The sample size is 750 without any lags, 705 with the immigrant stock lagged one year, 522 with the immigrant stock lagged five years and 293 with the immigrant stock lagged 10 years.

Table 5 shows the simple correlation between home country $i$'s immigrant stock in the United States $(IMM_i)$ and bilateral trade flows of country $i$ with the United States $(TRADE_i)$ without controlling for any country-specific aspects. This table shows how the overall trends in bilateral trade flows and immigrant stocks are correlated though time. As we can see from Table 5, all the three bilateral trade categories (aggregate, consumer, and producer goods) are positively correlated to immigration and lagged immigration. In fact, the correlation coefficients appear to be high ranging from 0.493 on U.S. bilateral trade in consumer goods to 0.663 on U.S. bilateral trade in producer products. The the correlation appears to peak with immigrants who entered the United States five years ago.

Table 5

U.S. Bilateral Trade Flows, Immigrant Stock, and Lagged Immigrant Stock

| Immigrant Stock | Aggregate *TRADE* | Consumer *TRADE* | Producer *TRADE* |
|---|---|---|---|
| Lag 0 year | 0.588 | 0.493 | 0.627 |
| Lag 1 year | 0.594 | 0.497 | 0.633 |
| Lag 5 years | 0.599 | 0.502 | 0.643 |
| Lag 10 years | 0.595 | 0.496 | 0.639 |

All correlations are significant at the 0.0001 significance level.

Table 6

Correlation Between Share of U.S. Bilateral Trade Flows, Share of Immigration, and Lagged Immigration

| Share of Immigrants | Aggregate $STRADE$ | Consumer $STRADE$ | Producer $STRADE$ |
|---|---|---|---|
| Lag 0 year | 0.646 | 0.587 | 0.641 |
| Lag 1 year | 0.648 | 0.588 | 0.692 |
| Lag 5 years | 0.653 | 0.594 | 0.701 |
| Lag 10 years | 0.649 | 0.589 | 0.699 |

All correlations are significant at the 0.0001 significance level.

It is also interesting to note that the highest correlation coefficients appear to be between producer goods trade and immigration. The positive and high correlation between immigration and bilateral trade flows in the different trade categories is suggestive of the immigrant link hypothesis; however, we must also keep in mind that this is only a bivariate examination, and many other factors that are related to immigration and trade have not been controlled for. For example, the relative sizes of the countries have not been controlled for, nor have other factors such as population or prices. It is reasonable to expect that because of size, large countries would have many immigrants in the United States and would also have large bilateral trade flows with the United States.

Table 6 shows the degree of correlation between the share of country $i$'s immigrants in the total immigrant stock of the United States ( $SIMM = IMM_i/IMM_{us}$) and the share of bilateral trade with home country $i$ in total trade of the United States ($STRADE = TRADE_i/TRADE_{us}$). This table indicates as to whether or not an increase in an immigrant community's share of the immigrant stock also implies an increase in the share bilateral trade in United States' total trade.As is shown, immigrant shares and trade shares are positively correlated. The correlation is high, in the range of 0.587 to 0.701. These results are favorable to the immigrant link hypothesis. However, as mentioned earlier, because other variables are not controlled for in this simple analysis, they must be seen as a preliminary result for the more in-depth regression analysis.

Table 7 is similar to Table 6 but gives a bit better indication of the relationship between immigration and bilateral trade flows by controlling for the size of the home countries' and the United States' world trade and the home countries' and United States' population. It shows the correlation between bilateral trade with home country $i$ relative to predicted trade

$$WTRADE = TRADE_i/pred(TRADE_i),$$

where, $pred(TRADE_i)=((TRADE_{i,W}*TRADE_{us,W})/TRADE_W)$, $TRADE_{i,W}$ is trade of the home country $i$ with the rest of the world, $TRADE_{us,W}$ is trade of the United States with the rest of the world, $TRADE_W$ is world trade, and the share of home country $i$'s immigrants in the total immigrant stock of the United States, $SIMM$, as defined above.

The value of $pred(TRADE_i)$ is simply calculated and is not estimated. In a sense, the variables $WTRADE$ indicates the unexplained movements in trade, and its correlation with $SIMM$ can provide us with some further evidence on the existence of immigrant links (immigrant links being the unexplained relationship between bilateral trade and the immigrant stock).From the table it can be seen that the correlation is positive for all trade categories. The correlations appear to be the strongest for scaled consumer trade, the highest correlation is 0.470 between immigrant share lagged 0 years and scaled consumer goods trade. Because world trade flows for the United States and home countries are controlled for here, the positive correlations shown here provide an even stronger suggestion of the immigrant link hypothesis than do the previous two tables.

Although the bivariate analysis is informative in that it gives an overall view of movements in scaled bilateral trade flows and share of the immigrant stocks using a simple model of predicted trade, it is difficult to determine whether or not the coincident movements in these variables are determined by immigrant links or are determined by other factors related to both. In the next

Table 7

Bilateral Trade Flows, Scaled Immigration, and Lagged Immigration

| Share of Imm. Stock | Aggregate $WTRADE$ | Consumer $WTRADE$ | Producer $WTRADE$ |
|---|---|---|---|
| Lag 0 year | 0.317 | 0.470 | 0.283 |
| Lag 1 year | 0.315 | 0.467 | 0.282 |
| Lag 5 years | 0.289 | 0.446 | 0.267 |
| Lag 10 years | 0.256 | 0.416 | 0.243 |

All correlations are significant at the 0.0001
significance level.

section, I move to a multiple regression analysis of the data in which more subtle distinctions between alternative hypotheses can be made.

## 5.4  REGRESSION ANALYSIS

The analysis in this section is designed to (1) distinguish the hypothesis of immigrant links against alternative hypotheses, (2) examine the roles that length of stay and the skill level of immigrants play in the immigrant-link effects, and (3) perform a sensitivity analysis of the immigrant-link effects. The following section calculates how much bilateral trade an additional immigrant will generate as a result of immigrant-link effects.

For the first task, I examine the relationship between immigration and bilateral export and import flows for aggregate, consumer, and producer manufactured goods flows. If immigration is found to influence only bilateral exports, then the immigrant preference for home country products hypothesis can be rejected in favor of the immigrant-link hypothesis. On the other hand, if imports are the only flow influenced by immigration, then probably the immigrant preference for home country products is the more relevant hypothesis. A combination of statistically significant and strong effects on both imports and exports may suggest a combination of these two hypotheses.[10]

### 5.4.1  *Immigrant Links*

Tables 8–10 show the estimation results for the U.S. bilateral trade flow equations. Because the equations are non-linear, they are estimated with the non-linear least squares regression technique.[11] Tables 18–20 in the appendix present the estimated country-specific intercepts for each trade equation. All variables are in logarithms except the immigrant information variable $[M_{us,j}/(\alpha_{10} + M_{us,j})]$, the immigrant skilled/unskilled ratio $(SKUK)$, and the length-of-stay variable $(STAY)$, which entered the equations as exponentials prior to the log transformation.

Table 8

Aggregate Trade Flows Between the United States and Home Countries

| Dependent Variable | Aggregate | |
| --- | --- | --- |
| | Exports | Imports |
| Lagged dependent variable | 0.624 | 0.472 |
| | (20.41) | (11.86) |
| Immigrant information | 4.960 | 1.928 |
| variable | (5.39) | (3.48) |
| Information sensitivity | 259 | 17890 |
| parameter | (0.62) | (2.64) |
| Immigrant skilled-unskilled | -0.034 | -0.037 |
| ratio | (-1.15) | (-0.85) |
| Immigrant stay | -0.033 | 0.042 |
| | (-1.47) | (1.24) |
| Immigrant stay$^2$ | 4.3E-3 | -1.5E-4 |
| | (1.05) | (-0.24) |
| Home country GDP | 0.154 | 0.052 |
| | (2.86) | (0.63) |
| Home country population | -0.720 | -0.754 |
| | (-3.04) | (-2.26) |
| U.S. GDP | 0.718 | 2.205 |
| | (1.60) | (3.30) |
| U.S. population | 4.100 | -3.457 |
| | (1.10) | (-0.55) |
| U.S. GDP deflator | -2.618 | -2.330 |
| | (-4.11) | (-2.69) |
| Home country GDP deflator | 0.003 | 0.038 |
| | (0.18) | (1.48) |
| U.S. export unit | 1.428 | |
| value index | (7.09) | |
| U.S. import unit | | 0.204 |
| value index | | (1.10) |
| Home country export unit | | -0.008 |
| value index | | (-0.15) |
| Home country import unit | -0.095 | |
| value index | (-2.51) | |
| $LM$ test for autocorrelation* | 1.42 | -0.36 |
| Adjusted $R^2$ | 0.998 | 0.997 |
| Observations | 716 | 708 |

NOTE: t-values are in parentheses.

*This is the t-value on $u_{t-1}$ in the modified $LM$ test for autocorrelation. See Harvey (1981, 274).

Table 9

Consumer Trade Flows Between the United States and Home Countries

| Dependent Variable | Consumer Exports | Imports |
|---|---|---|
| Lagged dependent variable | 0.686 | 0.736 |
| | (24.76) | (27.07) |
| Immigrant information variable | 4.069 | 3.554 |
| | (5.01) | (3.14) |
| Information sensitivity parameter | 377 | 1255 |
| | (0.75) | (1.14) |
| Immigrant skilled-unskilled ratio | -0.058 | -0.067 |
| | (-1.68) | (-1.29) |
| Immigrant stay | -0.021 | 0.018 |
| | (-0.81) | (0.45) |
| Immigrant stay$^2$ | 8.9E-5 | -1.1E-4 |
| | (0.19) | (-0.15) |
| Home country GDP | 0.143 | -0.133 |
| | (2.30) | (-1.46) |
| Home country population | -0.822 | 0.306 |
| | (-3.01) | (0.75) |
| U.S. GDP | 0.222 | 3.462 |
| | (0.43) | (4.47) |
| U.S. population | 9.227 | -12.363 |
| | (2.15) | (-1.72) |
| U.S. GDP deflator | -2.671 | -1.765 |
| | (-3.71) | (-1.76) |
| Home country GDP deflator | 0.014 | -0.016 |
| | (0.67) | (-0.53) |
| U.S. export unit value index | 1.352 | |
| | (5.83) | |
| U.S. import unit value index | | -.424 |
| | | (-1.97) |
| Home country export unit value index | | 0.004 |
| | | (0.06) |
| Home country import unit value index | -0.096 | |
| | (-2.22) | |
| *LM* test for autocorrelation* | 0.78 | -0.26 |
| Adjusted $R^2$ | 0.997 | 0.994 |
| Observations | 716 | 709 |

NOTE: t-values are in parentheses.
*This is the t-value on $u_{t-1}$ in the modified
*LM* test for autocorrelation. See Harvey (1981, 274).

## Table 10

Producer Trade Flows Between the United States and Home Countries

| Dependent Variable | Producer Exports | Imports |
|---|---|---|
| Lagged dependent variable | 0.532 | 0.378 |
| | (16.05) | (11.49) |
| Immigrant information | 3.991 | 1.412 |
| variable | (4.81) | (1.52) |
| Information sensitivity | 455 | 25210 |
| parameter | (0.77) | (0.97) |
| Immigrant skilled-unskilled | -0.099 | 0.140 |
| ratio | (-2.55) | (1.81) |
| Immigrant stay | -0.048 | -0.097 |
| | (-1.63) | (-1.69) |
| Immigrant stay$^2$ | 7.2E-4 | 0.001 |
| | (1.34) | (1.35) |
| Home country GDP | 0.205 | -0.027 |
| | (2.89) | (-0.19) |
| Home country population | -0.998 | -0.657 |
| | (-3.22) | (-1.09) |
| U.S. GDP | 0.207 | 2.691 |
| | (0.35) | (2.30) |
| U.S. population | 6.938 | 13.717 |
| | (1.42) | (1.23) |
| U.S. GDP deflator | -2.45 | -4.763 |
| | (-2.94) | (-3.15) |
| Home country GDP deflator | 0.007 | 0.076 |
| | (0.29) | (1.70) |
| U.S. export unit | 1.64 | |
| value index | (6.21) | |
| U.S. import unit | | 0.515 |
| value index | | (1.58) |
| Home country export unit | | -0.051 |
| value index | | (-0.56) |
| Home country import unit | -0.063 | |
| value index | (-1.28) | |
| *LM* test for autocorrelation* | 0.29 | 0.28 |
| Adjusted R$^2$ | 0.997 | 0.986 |
| Observations | 716 | 699 |

NOTE: t-values are in parentheses.

*This is the t-value on $u_{t-1}$ in the modified
*LM* test for autocorrelation. See Harvey (1981, 274).

The positive coefficients on the immigrant information variable across equations are consistent with the immigrant-link hypothesis. The coefficients on this variable range from 1.412 to 4.960, with the largest effects being in aggregate and consumer manufactured exports. The smallest coefficients on the immigrant information variable appear in the equations for imports in general and producer goods in particular. Because producer goods tend to be the least differentiated products (for instance, scrap metal) across countries, trade flows in these products may not benefit much from country-specific trade information. The immigrant information variable does not appear to be important in the producer imports equation. The size of the coefficient on this variable indicates the potential importance of immigrant information to bilateral trade flows. For example, comparing Brazil, with its average immigrant stock of 29,379 and an immigrant information factor in aggregate exports of 128.7 $(128.7 = e^{4.960 \times [29,379/(259+29,379)]})$, to Italy, with its average immigrant stock of 600,612 and an information factor of 142.3, the estimates indicate that Italy's trade with the United States due to immigrant links would be about 11 percent higher than Brazil's, *ceteris paribus*. In comparing Italy's trade with the United States to Tanzania's (Tanzania having the lowest immigrant stock in the sample at 1,301), the effects are even more dramatic. Here, Italy's trade due to immigrant links would be over twice that of Tanzania's.

The estimated immigrant information sensitivity parameter $(\vartheta)$ ranges from a value of 259 in the aggregate exports equation to 25,210 in the producer imports equation.[12] In general, the largest estimates of this parameter appear in the import equations. The larger this parameter is, the flatter the slope of the immigrant information function and the less sensitive the immigrant information variable to changes in the size of the immigrant stock. The high standard errors associated with this parameter suggest a wide range of possible values. In the maximum likelihood setting, this is indicative of a rather flat peak in the likelihood function in the direction of this parameter.

Estimates for the sensitivity parameters imply that 90 percent of the immigrant information effect will be exhausted at 12,016 immigrants for aggregate export flows and 370,879 immigrants for aggregate import flows.[13] Interestingly, most of these immigrant-link effects, although having a potentially large impact on exports, require a relatively small number of immigrants. In contrast with export flows, a relatively large number of immigrants are required before most of the immigrant-link effects are exhausted in import flows. The larger sensitivity parameter for imports may reflect the dominant role of immigrant preference for home country products, which tends to increase linearly with the flow of immigrants. On the other hand, in the export sector, immigrant information effects may dominate and then expire after a relatively small stock of immigrants is present. The estimated parameters indicate that there are 11 countries in the sample for which most of the immigrant-link effects in aggregate exports (due to the size of the immigrant stock) are not exhausted and 42 countries for which most of the immigrant-link effects in aggregate imports are not exhausted.[14]

The estimated parameters on the immigrant skilled–unskilled ratio are negative for all flows except in the producer imports equation. However, it does not appear that relative skill level has a strong significant effect on immigrant links. Two effects may be offsetting each other to different degrees. The first effect is the increase in foreign market information that accompanies skill level, which can have a positive effect on trade flows. The second effect is the possible propensity for highly skilled immigrants to create industries that are substitutes to traded goods, which may have a negative effect on trade. In this case, the second effect may be outweighing the first effect.

The estimated parameters on immigrant stay and squared immigrant stay indicate that for bilateral import flows, immigrant-link effects increase at a decreasing rate over time, whereas for exports they increase only after several years. For example, the estimated length-of-stay parameters in aggregate exports suggest that immigrant-link effects only increase after immigrants are in the United States for at least 3.8 years. This relationship suggests a possible time lag in the integration of immigrant links into the United States. Only after immigrants gain knowledge about the United States and are able to combine this with their home country contacts do immigrant-link effects grow. In aggregate imports, however, immigrant links increase from the beginning, but at a decreasing rate for the relevant time period. This relationship may reflect a positive preference for home country products that weakens as the immigrant stock ages. The role of length of stay in producer imports behaves in much the same way as it does in exports. Because of the importance of U.S. market information in this sector, only after a certain period of time do immigrant-link effects begin to increase. In general, however, the length-of-stay effects tend to be rather small and of low statistical significance.

Parameters estimated for the variables not associated with immigrant information conform, for the most part, to expectations. The coefficients on the lagged dependent variables fall between 0 and 1, and the coefficients on income of the importing country (that is, U.S. income in the import equations and country $j$'s income in the export equations) are positive and significant.

## 5.4.2  Sensitivity Analysis

How robust are the estimated immigrant-link effects? Tables 11–13 contain a sensitivity analysis of the estimated immigrant-link effects with respect to the specification of the immigrant-links variable and the inclusion of other potentially important determinates of trade.

Rows 1 and 2 of the tables show the estimated parameters of the immigrant information variable when the combined reciprocal stocks of foreign direct investment (FDI) and capital-to-capital distance are included in the basic estimating equations of Tables 8–10.[15] As the tables show, all of the previous results are robust to the inclusion of these additional variables. In fact, the size and significance level of the immigrant information variable increases in the producer imports equation, Table 13.[16]

In rows 2 and 4 of the tables, the sample is broken into English- and non-English-speaking countries, with distance between countries included. Most of the previous findings are robust to

Table 11

Sensitivity Analysis of Immigrant-Link Effects: Aggregate Trade

| Added variables | Immigrant-link Variable | Aggregate | |
|---|---|---|---|
| | | Exports | Imports |
| Combined | Immigrant info. var. | 4.342 | 1.298 |
| FDI | t-value | 4.71 | 2.44 |
| | Observations | 661 | 654 |
| | $R^2$ | 0.998 | 0.998 |
| Distance x | Immigrant info. var. | 4.959 | 1.928 |
| intercepts | t-value | 5.39 | 3.48 |
| | Observations | 716 | 708 |
| | $R^2$ | 0.998 | 0.997 |
| Distance x | Immigrant info. var. | 7.262 | 1.947 |
| intercepts | t-value | 3.17 | 0.01 |
| (English- | Observations | 152 | 149 |
| speakin countries*) | $R^2$ | 0.998 | 0.996 |
| Distance x | Immigrant info. var. | 3.696 | 1.466 |
| intercepts | t-value | 2.87 | 2.49 |
| (non-English- | Observations | 564 | 559 |
| speakin countries) | $R^2$ | 0.999 | 0.997 |
| None | Log of immigrant stock | 0.176 | 0.439 |
| | t-value | 1.94 | 3.14 |
| | Observations | 716 | 708 |
| | $R^2$ | 0.998 | 0.997 |

*English-speaking countries include: Australia, Canada,
India, Kenya, New Zealand, South Africa, Tanzania,
Trinidad and Tobago, the United Kingdom, and Zimbabwe.

Table 12

Sensitivity Analysis of Immigrant-Link Effects: Consumer Trade

| Added variables | Immigrant-link Variable | Consumer | |
|---|---|---|---|
| | | Exports | Imports |
| Combined | Immigrant info. var. | 4.023 | 6.556 |
| FDI | t-value | 4.70 | 3.07 |
| | Observations | 661 | 656 |
| | $R^2$ | 0.997 | 0.995 |
| Distance x | Immigrant info. var. | 4.069 | 3.554 |
| intercepts | t-value | 5.01 | 3.14 |
| | Observations | 665 | 709 |
| | $R^2$ | 0.997 | 0.994 |
| Distance x | Immigrant info. var. | 6.079 | 4.267 |
| intercepts | t-value | 3.44 | 1.30 |
| (English- | Observations | 152 | 148 |
| speakin countries*) | $R^2$ | 0.997 | 0.990 |
| Distance x | Immigrant info. var. | 3.195 | 5.291 |
| intercepts | t-value | 2.61 | 3.45 |
| (non-English- | Observations | 564 | 561 |
| speakin countries) | $R^2$ | 0.997 | 0.995 |
| None | Log of immigrant stock | 0.415 | 0.197 |
| | t-value | 3.74 | 1.18 |
| | Observations | 716 | 709 |
| | $R^2$ | 0.996 | 0.994 |

*English-speaking countries include: Australia, Canada,
India, Kenya, New Zealand, South Africa, Tanzania,
Trinidad and Tobago, the United Kingdom, and Zimbabwe.

Table 13

Sensitivity Analysis of Immigrant-Link Effects: Producer Trade

| Added variables | Immigrant-link Variable | Producer Exports | Imports |
|---|---|---|---|
| Combined | Immigrant info. var. | 7.066 | 1.831 |
| FDI | t-value | 4.33 | 2.04 |
| | Observations | 661 | 645 |
| | $R^2$ | 0.997 | 0.989 |
| Distance x | Immigrant info. var. | 3.991 | 1.411 |
| intercepts | t-value | 4.81 | 1.52 |
| | Observations | 716 | 699 |
| | $R^2$ | 0.997 | 0.986 |
| Distance x | Immigrant info. var. | 5.444 | 4.628 |
| intercepts | t-value | 3.22 | 2.028 |
| (English- | Observations | 152 | 148 |
| speakin countries*) | $R^2$ | 0.997 | 0.996 |
| Distance x | Immigrant info. var. | 3.345 | 1.035 |
| intercepts | t-value | 2.80 | 0.85 |
| (non-English- | Observations | 564 | 551 |
| speakin countries) | $R^2$ | 0.997 | 0.983 |
| None | Log of immigrant stock | 0.114 | 0.249 |
| | t-value | 0.91 | 1.03 |
| | Observations | 716 | 699 |
| | $R^2$ | 0.997 | 0.989 |

*English-speaking countries include: Australia, Canada,
India, Kenya, New Zealand, South Africa, Tanzania,
Trinidad and Tobago, the United Kingdom, and Zimbabwe.

this sample distinction, although it appears that immigrant links are not important in determining imports from English-speaking countries. Immigrant links do appear important, however, in determining imports from non-English-speaking countries. This makes sense if language is an import aspect of immigrant links. It may also reflect a greater immigrant preference for home country products if non-English-speaking immigrants have a stronger preference for their home country goods.

The last row in Tables 11–13 changes the specification of the immigrant information variable to be simply the log of the immigrant stock. Immigrant links in aggregate exports and imports and consumer exports remain robust to this specification; however, in consumer imports and producer exports and imports, they are sensitive to this change in specification. Because immigrants may begin to produce their own substitutes for home country products and because home country contacts may become less important as the size of the immigrant community grows large, a specification that allows for diminishing marginal benefits to immigrant links may be particularly important in these sectors.

## 5.5 THE MARGINAL EFFECT OF IMMIGRANT LINKS ON THE VALUE OF TRADE

Given the empirical results above, an interesting question is, How much trade does an additional immigrant generate? The extra exports and imports an additional immigrant would generate can be calculated using the estimates from the aggregate import and export equations in Table 8. The partial derivatives of these equations with respect to the immigrant stock are

$$\frac{\partial \log EX_{us,j}}{\partial M_{us,j}} = \frac{\alpha_9 \alpha_{10}}{(\alpha_{10} + M_{us,j})^2},$$

$$\frac{\partial \log IM_{j,us}}{\partial M_{us,j}} = \frac{\beta_9 \beta_{10}}{(\beta_{10} + M_{us,j})^2},$$

which imply the short-run increase in aggregate exports and imports generated by an additional immigrant in the last year of the sample is,

$$\frac{\partial EX_{us,j}}{\partial M_{us,j}} = \frac{\alpha_9 \alpha_{10}}{(\alpha_{10} + M_{us,j,1986})^2} \times EX_{us,j,1986},$$

$$\frac{\partial IM_{j,us}}{\partial M_{us,j}} = \frac{\beta_9 \beta_{10}}{(\beta_{10} + M_{us,j,1986})^2} \times IM_{us,j,1986},$$

where $EX_{us,j,1986}$ are aggregate exports from the United States to the home country $j$ in 1986, and $IM_{j,us,1986}$ are aggregate imports from the home country $j$ to the United States in 1986.

Using aggregate imports and exports in 1986, the immigrant stock in the United States, and the estimated parameters from Table 8, the value of exports and imports each additional immigrant generates is calculated and shown in Table 14.

Because this is a non-linear model, the largest dollar increases in bilateral trade flows from an additional immigrant are not necessarily from countries that have large immigrant stocks in the United States. The largest marginal immigrant-link effects are from countries with relatively small immigrant stocks and a large potential for trade. For example, these calculations suggest that an additional immigrant from Singapore has the largest potential to generate new trade, with additional imports at a value of $29,359 per year and exports at a value of $47,708. On the other hand, an additional immigrant from the Philippines would create only about $6 of imports per year and $4 of exports.

Table 14

Dollar Value Increase in Bilateral Trade from One Additional Immigrant in 1986

| | Immigrant Stock | Imports Estimate | t-value* | Exports Estimate | t-value |
|---|---|---|---|---|---|
| Australia | 38.104 | $ 2,507 | 2.32737 | $ 4,844 | 2.12801 |
| Austria | 113,143 | 91 | 2.71657 | 46 | 2.06962 |
| Brazil | 43,133 | 5,007 | 3.25376 | 2,650 | 2.11758 |
| Canada | 806,385 | 136 | 2.33452 | 89 | 2.04488 |
| Colombia | 156,295 | 107 | 2.59879 | 69 | 2.06163 |
| Cyprus | 7,258 | 275 | 2.85329 | 1,218 | 2.56701 |
| Denmark | 37,634 | 1,672 | 3.33443 | 678 | 2.12914 |
| El Salvador[1] | 85,422 | 71 | 2.84691 | 75 | 2.07908 |
| Ethiopia[2] | 6,640 | 2,453 | 2.78929 | 9,940 | 2.62566 |
| Finland | 26,877 | 1,720 | 3.47879 | 665 | 2.16607 |
| France | 115,802 | 1,009 | 2.70700 | 688 | 2.06896 |
| Greece | 176,386 | 18 | 2.56257 | 18 | 2.05925 |
| Hungary | 114,124 | 24 | 2.71300 | 10 | 2.06937 |
| Iceland | 4,771 | 12,625 | 2.57885 | 3,061 | 2.92062 |
| India | 298,673 | 35 | 2.44453 | 22 | 2.05170 |
| Ireland | 154,579 | 56 | 2.60230 | 77 | 2.06186 |
| Israel | 72,156 | 614 | 2.93801 | 548 | 2.08622 |
| Italy | 634,702 | 36 | 2.35217 | 15 | 2.04596 |
| Japan | 192,139 | 2,965 | 2.53924 | 933 | 2.05773 |
| Jordan | 31,063 | 14 | 3.42979 | 435 | 2.14854 |
| Kenya[3] | 7,299 | 2,239 | 2.85743 | 2,174 | 2.56353 |
| Malaysia | 15,652 | 12,857 | 3.40579 | 8,775 | 2.26300 |
| Malta | 8,476 | 593 | 2.97045 | 412 | 2.48004 |
| Morocco[3] | 8,231 | 779 | 2.94787 | 4,973 | 2.49516 |
| Netherlands | 89,069 | 702 | 2.82581 | 1,263 | 2.07749 |
| New Zealand | 12,964 | 8,060 | 3.29224 | 6,469 | 2.31352 |
| Nicaragua[2] | 34,320 | 243 | 3.38369 | 268 | 2.13796 |
| Norway | 55,775 | 479 | 3.09239 | 383 | 2.09982 |

(continued)

| | Immigrant Stock | Imports Estimate | t-value* | Exports Estimate | t-value |
|---|---|---|---|---|---|
| Pakistan | 55,804 | 144 | 3.09207 | 339 | 2.09979 |
| Philippines | 668,591 | 6 | 2.34797 | 4 | 2.04570 |
| S. Africa | 20,091 | 7,860 | 3.49240 | 3,593 | 2.21094 |
| Singapore[2] | 4,180 | 29,359 | 2.50766 | 47,708 | 3.08533 |
| S. Korea | 186,163 | 499 | 2.54765 | 235 | 2.05828 |
| Spain | 70,173 | 765 | 2.95392 | 677 | 2.08752 |
| Sri Lanka | 6,543 | 10,466 | 2.77897 | 1,838 | 2.63606 |
| Sweden | 73,150 | 1,105 | 2.93029 | 446 | 2.08559 |
| Switzerland | 39,562 | 4,347 | 3.30573 | 2,411 | 2.12471 |
| Syria | 22,116 | 23 | 3.50173 | 152 | 2.19451 |
| Tanzania[2] | 2,160 | 7,529 | 2.25135 | 13,521 | 4.62691 |
| Thailand | 111,076 | 194 | 2.72430 | 97 | 2.07016 |
| Trinidad[3] | 68,602 | 353 | 2.96700 | 136 | 2.08861 |
| Tunisia | 2,816 | 1,548 | 2.33647 | 22,100 | 3.83784 |
| Turkey[1] | 47,182 | 265 | 3.19785 | 173 | 2.11083 |
| U.K. | 613,804 | 55 | 2.35499 | 39 | 2.04614 |
| W. Germany | 681,692 | 72 | 2.34646 | 29 | 2.04561 |
| Yugoslavia[4] | 112,573 | 36 | 2.68434 | 49 | 2.06739 |
| Zimbabwe | 3,777 | 5,795 | 2.45801 | 4,218 | 3.23648 |

NOTE— Import and export data are in U.S. dollars.
Last year available is: 1984[1], 1980[2], 1985[3], 1983[4].
*See Fomby, Hill, and Johnson (1984, 58) for a discussion of the Delta method that was used to calculate the standard errors and t-values.

## 5.6 SUMMARY

This chapter investigates an aspect of immigration that, until now, has received little attention—the foreign market knowledge that immigrants naturally embody. Immigrants convey knowledge spillovers that can reduce information costs to economic agents who do not migrate. These spillovers reveal value-creating production and trade opportunities and utility-increasing consumption opportunities for the non-migrants in both countries.

The empirical results indicate that immigrant information can play an important role in determining U.S. bilateral trade flows. The effects of immigrant information appear to be stronger in the exports and imports of consumer manufactured products than in the exports and imports of producer goods. Overall, exports appear to be influenced the most by immigrant links, while imports are influenced the least.

Although immigrant-link effects are the strongest in the export sector, a relatively small immigrant community can exhaust most of these effects. However, a relatively large community is required before most of the effects are exhausted in the import sector. This finding may reflect the dominant role that immigrant preference for home country products plays in the import sector.

Several interesting facets of immigrant links remain to be explored. One particularly relevant issue is whether immigrant links lead to an increase in the worldwide transfer of technology. This question is especially relevant in light of the recent work in endogenous growth and the international diffusion of knowledge.[17]

# NOTES

[1] For a discussion of the necessary and sufficient conditions for substitution or complementarity, see Wong (1986a).

[2] See Leamer (1990), Jovanovic and Rob (1989), Lucus (1988), and Rauch (1991).

[3] But even in the case of the immigrant preference hypothesis with direct effects on imports, an indirect effect on exports may result as well if trade flows tend to be balanced. However, in a world with functioning capital markets and convertible currencies, the trade account between any two countries does not necessarily have to be balanced in the short or long run.

[4] The constant $A$ disappears because it enters multiplicatively on each side of the equation.

[5] A sensitivity analysis was performed using a bilateral exchange rate variable instead of unit import and export prices. The effect on the standard error of the immigrant links variable did not change enough to alter the previous statistical inferences about the immigrant links effect.

[6] Bergstrand (1985) makes similar approximations for these price terms.

[7] The robustness of this specification is examined in the following section. A potential bias may arise from using country-specific dummy variables to account for differences in factor endowments because immigration itself influences factor endowments. The bias created by the correlation between regressors is probably very minor, given that immigration from any one country as a percentage of the total U.S. population is very small. For example, the total Canadian immigrant population in the United States (the largest in the sample) represents less than 0.4 percent of the total U.S. population, and immigration in any one year represents a much smaller faction of the change in U.S. total population.

[8] Annual data were collected for 47 U.S. trading partners for 1970 through 1986. The data were treated as pooled cross-section time-series data, and inclusion of a country in the data set was based solely on the availability of all data. Aggregate trade data are constructed from the International Monetary Fund (IMF) *Direction of Trade Statistics*. Trade data on consumer and producer manufactured imports and exports are derived from the Organization for Economic Cooperation and Development (OECD) statistics on trade in manufactured goods. The 1980 U.S. census and the Immigration and Naturalization Service (INS) public-use data on yearly immigration provide annual information on the stock of immigrants in the United States and their skill levels and length of stay. Income, prices, and population are extracted from the IMF's

*International Financial Statistics.* A complete description of the data is shown in the appendix.

[9] A full description of the data can be found in the appendix.

[10] In the estimated equations, the direction of causality is assumed to be from immigration to trade. The basis for this assumption is threefold. First, U.S. immigration flows are subject to binding quotas, which, in addition to the preference given to family reunification, makes them much more of an exogenously determined variable than bilateral trade flows. Second, case studies of various immigrant communities suggest that individual migration decisions are primarily determined by wage differentials and the size of the existing immigrant community, rather than the size of trade flows. Finally, in a separate analysis using Granger-causality tests, I found evidence that suggests immigration causes trade. In Granger-causality tests, immigration preceded trade for 22 trading partners, trade preceded immigration for 11 trading partners, and immigration moved coincidentally with trade, or causality could not be determined, for 14 trading partners. Of course, the degrees of freedom for any one country are extremely low (at most 12), which weakens the ability to make strong statistical inferences with regard to temporal precedence.

[11] I used the NLIN procedure in SAS to estimate the parameters of this model. Starting from good guesses of the parameters obtained from a double-log approximation of this model, the procedure iteratively finds the value of all parameters that minimizes the SSE of the equation. Different starting values of the parameters were used to find a global minimum.

[12] This variable was constrained during estimation to be greater than or equal to zero.

[13] As an example of how this number is calculated for aggregate exports, $4.960[M_{us,j}/(259+M_{us,j})] = \log[(e^{4.960}-1)\times.90+1]$ implies $M_{us,j} = 12,016$.

[14] The countries in the exports sector are Cyprus, Ethiopia, Iceland, Kenya, Malta, Morocco, Singapore, Sri Lanka, Tanzania, Tunisia, and Zimbabwe. In the imports sector, all countries in the sample are included except Canada, Italy, the Philippines, the United Kingdom, and West Germany.

[15] Distance is interacted with the country-specific intercepts. Foreign direct investment was specifically included in the analysis because it may contain the same type of information effects as immigrant links.

[16] Yearly data on the reciprocal stocks of foreign direct investment were derived from the U.S. Bureau of Economic Analysis Benchmark Surveys. The foreign direct investment stocks were not found to be significant in determining trade flows, but their average values over 1970–86 were found to be significant. This is probably due to the year-to-year volatility of measured foreign direct in-

vestment stocks. Reported foreign direct investment stocks can change rapidly from year to year (and can sometimes be negative), even though a long-term investment presence in the country remains fairly constant. Foreign investment may appear to be volatile because of reverse debt agreements between foreign and domestic affiliates of the same company.

[17] See, for example, Romer (1990) or Grossman and Helpman (1991).

# Chapter 6

# Conclusion

This book has examined an aspect of international labor migration that has received little attention in the formal economic literature, namely, the close ties or links that immigrant communities maintain with their home countries and the trade-enhancing effect this can have on bilateral trade flows between the host country and the home country. The primary question addressed is, Do immigrant links to the home country affect the bilateral trade flows between the home and host countries? This investigation is conducted at both a theoretical and empirical level. In this chapter, the content of the previous chapters is reviewed, the conclusions stated and the policy implications are discussed.

## 6.1 OVERVIEW

The literature review in chapter 2 demonstrated that the study of immigration and trade is by no means a new subject, but until now, the study of immigration as a source of increasing trade linkages between countries has not been more than a casual speculation. The immigrant network and immigrant entrepreneur literature has provided several case studies of groups that have taken advantage of their particular knowledge of home country markets and home country contacts to engage in trading activities. The approach to immigration taken in this book is that these linkages and networks can have general effects on imports and exports as the total amount of foreign market information and trade contacts increase between the host and home countries. Traditional factor endowment models of trade, while allowing for immigration and trade to be complementary, do not predict a relationship between bilateral trade and immigration once factor endowments are controlled for. Empirically, one study, Wong (1986b) found a positive relationship between immigration and total trade flows although no analysis of bilateral trade flows and immigration was analyzed. Studies of immigration and its impact on native wages have found little evidence that immigration puts a large downward pressure on domestic wages. This study finds a strong positive relationship between bilateral flows of exports and immigration and a weak positive relationship between immigration and bilateral flows of imports. Immigrant links, by having a positive effect on the tradables sector, may explain to some degree the small impact of immigration on natives' wages.

In chapter 3, a general equilibrium model of trade was developed that incorporated the hypothesis that immigrants increase foreign market information and decrease the transactions costs to trade between the host and home countries. The analysis took the point of view of a developed economy that receives an inflow of labor. Two conclusions of the model contrast sharply against those of the standard 2X2 Heckscher-Ohlin-Samuelson trade model. First, although the model has only two traded goods and two factors, immigration can have a positive effect on trade. The difference between the immigrant link model and the standard model due to the existence of a distortion, which is the lack of foreign market information, that decreases with immigrant links to the home country. Secondly, because the distortion is reduced with immigration, the host country also experiences and increase in welfare.

The effects of immigration and immigrant links on factor rewards were also discussed in this chapter. It was shown that in the medium run with capital sector-specific and labor mobile, immigration alone tends to decrease wages, as is the case in the specific factors model. However, with a decrease in transactions costs due to immigrant links, the tradables sector expands, which tends to mitigate the downward pressure on wages.

In chapter 4, a specific case of the general model was developed as a framework to empirically examine immigrants links. In this model, goods are differentiated by country of origin and consumers' utility depends on the variety of goods available. By supplying foreign market information immigrants decrease the transactions costs to trade between the host and home countries. The decrease in transactions costs, in turn, results in a decrease in the wedge between the foreign and domestic price of traded goods and an increase in bilateral trade flows.

Chapter 5 is an empirical analysis into the immigrant link hypothesis and begins by considering how immigrant links can be distinguished from other alternative hypotheses that also make predictions for the relationship between immigration and trade. Out of this discussion, several aspects of the immigrant link hypothesis were found to be distinct enough to allow for an empirical investigation into the question with the data available. First, a positive relationship between immigration and bilateral trade flows, controlling for endowments between countries, would support the immigrant links hypothesis over other models of trade. Furthermore, a positive correlation between immigration and bilateral imports and exports (especially exports) would provide an indication as to the relevance of the immigrant link hypothesis over simply the immigrant preference for home-country products hypothesis.

Several questions concerning how immigrant characteristics influence immigrant links were also raised in chapter 5. The chapter addressed such questions as, How does the skill level of immigrants influence immigrant links? Does a longer length of stay in the host country imply a strengthening or weakening of immigrant links? What roles do language and regional proximity to other countries play in influencing immigrant links?

Using a panel data set that consisted of 47 U.S. trading partners and data on the types of products that are traded, the size and source country distribution of the immigrant stock and immigrant characteristics, the immigrant link hypothesis was evaluated.

The results indicate that immigrant links can indeed play an important role in determining bilateral trade flows. The effects of immigrant links seem to be stronger in the exports and imports of consumer manufactured products than in the exports and imports of producer goods. Overall, exports appear to be influenced the most by immigrant links, while imports are influenced the least. When modeling immigrant link effects as a linear function of the immigrant stock, the results indicate that, holding all other factors constant, a 10 percent increase in a country's immigrant stock in the United States will lead to about a 2.5 percent increase in aggregate exports and a 2 percent increase in imports. Of course, when the immigrant links are modeled as a non-linear function of the immigrant stock the effects can be much more dramatic between countries. For example, comparing Brazil, with its average immigrant stock of 29,379, to Italy, with its average immigrant stock of 600,612, the model estimates that Italy's trade with the United States due to immigrant links would be about 11 percent higher than Brazil's, *ceteris paribus*. In comparing Italy's trade with the United States to Tanzania's (Tanzania having the lowest immigrant stock in the sample at 1,301), the effects are even more dramatic. Here, Italy's trade due to immigrant-links would be over twice that of Tanzania's.

The estimated parameters on the immigrant skilled–unskilled ratio did not appear to be that significant in affecting immigrant links. Two effects may be offsetting each other to different degrees. The first effect is the increase in foreign market information that accompanies skill level, which can have a positive effect on trade flows. The second effect is the possible propensity for highly skilled immigrants to create industries that are substitutes to traded goods, which may have a negative effect on trade. In this case, the second effect may be outweighing the first effect.

The empirical results suggest that a large immigrant community is not required to exhaust most of the benefits of immigrant links in the exports sectors. However, a large immigrant community is required before most of the benefits of immigrant links in the imports sector are exhausted. This may reflect the dominant role of immigrant preference for home country products in the import sectors that tends to increase linearly with the flow of immigrants. On the other hand, in the export sectors, immigrant information effects may dominate and then tend to expire after a relatively small stock of immigrants is present. The empirical analysis indicates that 90 percent of the immigrant link effects are exhausted in the exports sector after the immigrant stock reaches a size of about 12,000 immigrants and in the imports sector after the immigrant stock reaches a size of about 370,000 immigrants. Of course, these are average estimates and for each home country the values would depend on the potential for trade and size of the home country.

The estimated parameters on immigrant stay indicate that for bilateral import flows, immigrant-link effects increase at a decreasing rate over time, whereas for exports they increase only after several years. For example, the estimated length-of-stay parameters in aggregate exports suggest that immigrant-link effects only increase after immigrants are in the United States for at least 3.8 years. This relationship suggests a possible time lag in the integration of immigrant links into the United States. Only after immigrants gain knowledge about the United States and are able to combine this with their home country contacts do immigrant-link effects grow. In aggregate imports, however, immigrant links increase from the beginning, but at a decreasing rate for the relevant time period. This relationship may reflect a positive preference for home country products that weakens as the immigrant stock ages. In general, however, the length-of-stay effects tend to be rather small and of low statistical significance.

The empirical results suggest that the immigrant link effects on imports rise slowly over a large range in the stock of immigrants, while the effects on exports rise quickly over a short range in the stock of immigrants. Although it makes sense to think of the effects on imports as being primarily due to immigrant preference for home country products that rises slowly as the immigrant stock increases and the effects on exports as being due to immigrant information effects that rise quickly and then level off, an important question is why don't the effects on imports rise faster than exports reflecting both an information effect and immigrant preference effect? In other words, if information effects and immigrant preference effects are both present, why don't we observe an greater additive effect on imports?

A possible explanation for this is that the foreign market information requirements are greater for exports than imports. The difference in information requirements being due to the nature of exporting and importing activities. While exporting requires a knowledge of foreign distribution networks, foreign preferences, and guarantees of payment upon delivery, importing may only require a knowledge of foreign products, domestic preferences, and domestic distribution networks. Consequently, the foreign information requirements may be higher for exporting than importing.

Questions related to the role that language and regional proximity play in the immigrant links hypothesis were also examined empirically. The analysis found that immigrant links are not important in determining imports from English-speaking countries. Immigrant links do appear important, however, in determining imports from non-English-speaking countries. This makes sense if language is an important aspect of immigrant links. It may also reflect a greater immigrant preference for home country products if non-English-speaking immigrants have a stronger preference for their home country goods.

Distance also is important in determining bilateral trade flows, but so are immigrant links. Controlling for distance between countries in the bilateral trade model did not eliminate immigrant links effects; neither did foreign direct investment between countries.

Using estimates from the non-linear bilateral trade model to calculate dollar increases in bilateral trade flows from an additional immigrant, it was found that the largest marginal immigrant link effects are from countries with a relatively small immigrant stock and a large potential for trade. For example, the empirical results suggest that an additional immigrant from Singapore has the largest potential to generate trade, at a value of about \$80,000 per year. On the other hand, an additional immigrant from the Philippines would only create only about \$10 worth of trade per year.

## 6.2 POLICY IMPLICATIONS

What does this research mean for immigration policy? How should a country conduct its immigration policy, knowing that immigrant links exist? Prior to the discussion in this book, the total number of immigrants to be admitted and their skill level were the only factors considered to be economically important. Questions concerning the source country of immigrants have generally not been given any attention by economists and, in terms of policy, have largely been driven by society's tendency toward xenophobia, as seen in the limitations placed on Asian immigration in the earlier part of this century. Certainly, immigration questions concerning refugees and the preference of admitting family members cannot be addressed in this context, but a policy consistent with maximizing immigrant link benefits can be implemented.

With regard to increasing the total flow of immigrants and immigration's effects on natives' wages, the theory developed here suggests that the negative impact on natives' wages may be mitigated to a degree by immigrant links. The results of previous empirical studies, which have found a small effect on natives' wages from immigration, could well be due to these immigrant link effects. Of course, a full econometric study would have to be undertaken to determine the role of immigrant links in influencing natives' wages, but a policy that increases the diversity of the stock of immigrants may have less of a negative impact on individuals that compete the most with immigrants. Consequently, increasing immigration from countries that provide the largest immigrant links would increase host country welfare and might even have less of an impact on domestic wages than increasing immigration from countries that provide fewer immigrant links.

This analysis suggests that the greatest welfare benefits from immigration could be derived by allowing increased immigration from those countries in which the immigrant link effects are the highest. In other words, a policy prescription for the United States indicated by the analysis is to promote diversity in the immigrant stock. This could be done by allowing free immigration from countries that have a high potential to create trade through immigrant linkages (for example, immigrants from Singapore because they are relatively small population in the United States, and their home country has a large potential for trade).

These policy prescriptions would entail significant changes in the way the United States approaches immigration, which may or may not be politically feasible. First, it would mean that future immigration from a particular country would depend on the current levels of its immigrant stock in the United States. This policy already exists *de facto* in the United States, but operates contrary to the immigrant link hypothesis. In the present system, immediate family members of U.S. citizens are exempt from numerical limitations on immigration, and other close family members are given priority in the overall numerically limited preference categories. So, if a country has a high present level of immigration, future immigration will also be high as family members are carried over on a previous immigrant's visa. In this system, future immigrants are pushed aside by immigrants from other, higher demand countries unless the first country's demand for immigrant visas remains stable relative to other countries'. For immigration policy to be consistent with maximizing the benefits of immigrant links, future immigration from a particular country must increase as the size of present immigrant population falls. Without modifying the current family preference system, this policy would indicate relaxing the numerical limitations for certain countries with the highest immigrant link effects.

A number of interesting facets of the relationship between immigration and immigrant links remain to be explored. A particularly useful research project would be an examination of differences in the domestic wage response to increases in immigration from different immigrant source countries. The question to be addressed is whether an increase in the size of immigrant communities with the largest immigrant link effects has the smallest effects on natives' wages. The results would provide useful information on the ability of a host country to increase immigration without placing a large burden on natives who compete the most with immigrants.

Another interesting area for future research is an examination of the relationship between skilled immigration and entrepreneurial activity. This analysis could help determine if, indeed, skilled immigrants are more apt to create industries in the host country that provides substitute products for home country goods. An analysis of this sort would be extremely useful in understanding the relationship between immigrant links and skilled immigration.

Finally, an investigation into the possible asymmetries in foreign market information requirements in exporting and importing activities would be helpful. By determining the size of these asymmetries, a better distinction between immigrant link effects and immigrant preference for home country product effects can be made.

# Appendix

*Data Sources.* Annual data were collected for 47 U.S. trading partners for 1970 through 1986. The data were treated as pooled cross-section time-series data, and inclusion of a country in the data set was based solely on the availability of all data. Table 15 lists these countries and the years of available data for each. Given the wide variety of countries in the sample, I do not expect a systematic bias due to country selection.

Aggregate trade data on exports and imports are constructed from the International Monetary Fund (IMF) Direction of Trade Statistics. Trade data on consumer and producer manufactured imports and exports are derived from the Organization for Economic Cooperation and Development (OECD) statistics on trade in manufactured goods. All nominal variables are in millions of U.S. dollars.

In constructing the trade data, a problem arises in distinguishing between consumer goods and producer goods because the ultimate end-use of manufactured imports and exports is unknown. I based the distinction here on a selection from the four-digit International Standard Industrial Classification (ISIC) codes. For example, jewelry and bicycles are classified as consumer goods, while scrap metal, engines, and turbines are classified as producer products. Some goods, however, do not seem to fit nicely into these two simple categories, such as non-metallic mineral products and computing and accounting machinery. I attempted to exclude ambiguous categories of goods from the analysis. However, the inability to know the exact end-use of all types of goods may add some degree of error to the analysis.

The 1980 census and the Immigration and Naturalization Service (INS) public-use data on yearly immigration provide annual information on the stock of immigrants in the United States and their skill levels. A source of difficulty in estimating the actual stock of immigrants on a yearly basis is the problem of under-counting due to illegal immigration and over-counting due to emigration.

Although the 1980 census includes some illegal immigrants, Greenwood (1983) estimates that more than 2 million immigrants are excluded from the count. Furthermore, I constructed the data after 1980 from yearly INS information that completely excludes illegal immigration. Emigration is accounted for, to some degree, by comparing the date of arrival reported in the 1980 census with the INS information on yearly immigration flows.

Skilled workers are defined as immigrants whose occupation is classified as "professional, technical, and kindred workers." Unskilled workers are those whose occupation is classified as "general machine operators," "laborers," "farm workers," or "service workers."

I constructed the average length of stay of the immigrants from dates of entry into the United States in the 1970–86 period. Consequently, the measure is the average length of stay of the immigrants who arrived between 1970 and 1986. Because decreases in the immigrant stock from return emigration or death could not be estimated, this variable may overestimate the average length of stay for immigrant communities that experienced most of their growth in the earlier part of this period. The immigrant communities that tend to have the longer lengths of stay are from European countries, whereas those with the shortest lengths of stay are mostly from African, Asian, and Latin American countries.

I extracted data on income, prices, and population from the IMF's International Financial Statistics. Income is in millions of U.S. dollars, and prices are export and import unit value indexes that are scaled to equal 100 in 1985.

Because the choice of countries for the analysis was based solely on the availability of data, some important immigration countries may have been excluded from the analysis. For example, Mexico is excluded from the analysis because data on its unit-value export and import prices are not available. The exclusion of Mexico, however, may be desirable for the empirical analysis because, although it is an important source of U.S. immigrants, its situation is special in that it shares a border with the United States and has an immigrant stock that is far above that of all other countries.

Table 15

U.S. Bilateral Trading Partners and Years of Available Data

| | |
|---|---|
| Australia | 1970-1986 |
| Austria | 1970-1986 |
| Brazil | 1970-1986 |
| Canada | 1970-1986 |
| Colombia | 1970-1986 |
| Cyprus | 1970-1986 |
| Denmark | 1970-1986 |
| El Salvador | 1970-1984 |
| Ethiopia | 1970-1980 |
| Finland | 1970-1986 |
| France | 1970-1986 |
| Greece | 1970-1986 |
| Hungary | 1970-1986 |
| Iceland | 1970-1986 |
| India | 1970-1986 |
| Ireland | 1970-1986 |
| Israel | 1970-1986 |
| Italy | 1970-1986 |
| Japan | 1970-1986 |
| Jordan | 1970-1986 |
| Kenya | 1970-1985 |
| Malaysia | 1970-1986 |
| Malta | 1970-1986 |
| Morocco | 1970-1985 |
| Netherlands | 1970-1986 |
| New Zealand | 1970-1986 |

(continued)

| | |
|---|---|
| Nicaragua | 1970-1980 |
| Norway | 1970-1986 |
| Pakistan | 1970-1986 |
| Philippines | 1970-1986 |
| South Africa | 1970-1986 |
| South Korea | 1970-1986 |
| Singapore | 1972-1980 |
| Spain | 1970-1986 |
| Sri Lanka | 1970-1986 |
| Sweden | 1970-1986 |
| Switzerland | 1970-1986 |
| Syria | 1970-1986 |
| Tanzania | 1970-1980 |
| Thailand | 1970-1986 |
| Trinidad | 1970-1985 |
| Tunisia | 1970-1986 |
| Turkey | 1970-1984 |
| United Kingdom | 1970-1986 |
| West Germany | 1970-1986 |
| Yugoslavia | 1970-1983 |
| Zimbabwe | 1970-1986 |

Table 16

| ISIC | Consumer Manufactured Products |
|------|-------------------------------|
| | Description |
| 3111 | Preserved meat products |
| 3112 | Dairy products |
| 3113 | Canned fruits and vegetables |
| 3114 | Canned and preserved fish |
| 3117 | Bakery products |
| 3119 | Cocoa and sugar confectionery |
| 3132 | Wine products |
| 3133 | Malt liquors and malt |
| 3134 | Soft drinks and carbonated waters |
| 3140 | Tobacco manufactures |
| 3212 | Textiles excluding wearing apparel |
| 3220 | Wearing apparel |
| 3232 | Leather product excluding footwear |
| 3240 | Leather footwear |
| 3312 | Cane containers and small cane ware |
| 3320 | Wood furniture and fixtures |
| 3523 | Soap and cosmetics |
| 3610 | Pottery, china, and earthware |
| 3620 | Glass products |
| 3811 | Cutlery and general hardware |
| 3812 | Metal furniture and fixtures |
| 3819 | Metal products excluding machinery and equipment |
| 3832 | Radio and TV equipment and apparatus |
| 3833 | Electric appliances and housewares |
| 3843 | Motor vehicles |
| 3844 | Motorcycles and bicycles |
| 3852 | Photographic and optical goods |
| 3853 | Watches and clocks |
| 3901 | Jewelry |
| 3902 | Musical instruments |
| 3903 | Sporting goods |

Table 17

## Producer Manufactured Products

| ISIC | Description |
|------|-------------|
| 3122 | Prepared animal feeds |
| 3211 | Weaving and finishing textiles |
| 3213 | Knitting mills |
| 3215 | Rope and twine industries |
| 3232 | Fur dressing and dyeing industries |
| 3313 | Sawmills, planing, and other wood mills |
| 3411 | Pulp and paper |
| 3412 | Paper boxes and paperboard |
| 3511 | Basic industrial chemicals |
| 3512 | Fertilizers and pesticides |
| 3513 | Synthetic resins and plastic |
| 3521 | Paints, varnishes, and lacquers |
| 3522 | Drugs and medicines |
| 3530 | Petroleum products |
| 3540 | Miscellaneous petroleum and coal products |
| 3551 | Tire and tubes industries |
| 3692 | Cement, lime, and plaster |
| 3699 | Nonmetallic mineral products |
| 3710 | Iron and steel basic industries |
| 3801 | Metal scrap |
| 3813 | Structural metal products |
| 3821 | Engines and turbines |
| 3822 | Agricultural machinery |
| 3823 | Metal and woodworking machinery |
| 3824 | Industry machinery, excluding 3823 |
| 3825 | Office, computing, and accounting machinery |
| 3831 | Electric industrial machinery |
| 3841 | Shipbuilding and repairing |
| 3842 | Railroad equipment |
| 3845 | Aircraft |
| 3849 | Transportation equipment |
| 3851 | Scientific equipment |

Table 18

Country-Specific Intercepts: Aggregate Trade Equations

| | Aggregate | | | |
| | Exports | | Imports | |
| Country | Est. | *t*-val. | Est. | *t*-val. |
|---|---|---|---|---|
| Australia | -40.63 | -2.29 | -11.69 | -0.40 |
| Austria | -41.79 | -2.36 | -13.80 | -0.47 |
| Brazil | -39.24 | -2.22 | -9.60 | -0.33 |
| Canada | -39.52 | -2.23 | -10.75 | -0.37 |
| Colombia | -40.61 | -2.29 | -11.72 | -0.40 |
| Cyprus | -43.70 | -2.45 | -16.27 | -0.55 |
| Denmark | -41.84 | -2.36 | -13.31 | -0.45 |
| El Salvador | -42.08 | -2.37 | -13.30 | -0.45 |
| Ethiopia | -40.98 | -2.31 | -11.46 | -0.39 |
| Finland | -42.10 | -2.37 | -13.55 | -0.46 |
| France | -39.76 | -2.25 | -10.98 | -0.37 |
| Greece | -41.52 | -2.34 | -13.72 | -0.47 |
| Hungary | -41.87 | -2.37 | -14.34 | -0.49 |
| Iceland | -44.48 | -2.49 | -15.16 | -0.51 |
| India | -38.37 | -2.17 | -9.04 | -0.31 |
| Ireland | -41.97 | -2.36 | -14.43 | -0.49 |
| Israel | -41.52 | -2.33 | -12.90 | -0.44 |
| Italy | -39.80 | -2.25 | -11.25 | -0.38 |
| Japan | -38.89 | -2.20 | -9.42 | -0.32 |
| Jordan | -42.26 | -2.38 | -15.53 | -0.53 |
| Kenya | -41.51 | -2.34 | -12.12 | -0.41 |
| Malaysia | -40.92 | -2.31 | -10.79 | -0.37 |
| Malta | -44.26 | -2.48 | -16.92 | -0.57 |
| Morocco | -40.84 | -2.31 | -12.94 | -0.44 |
| Netherlands | -40.37 | -2.28 | -12.43 | -0.42 |
| New Zealand | -42.12 | -2.37 | -12.78 | -0.43 |
| Nicaragua | -42.47 | -2.39 | -13.76 | -0.47 |
| Norway | -41.93 | -2.36 | -13.61 | -0.46 |

(continued)

| Country | Aggregate Exports Est. | *t*-val. | Imports Est. | *t*-val. |
|---|---|---|---|---|
| Pakistan | -40.02 | -2.26 | -11.14 | -0.38 |
| Philippines | -40.20 | -2.27 | -11.29 | -0.38 |
| S. Africa | -40.42 | -2.28 | -10.62 | -0.36 |
| S. Korea | -40.16 | -2.27 | -10.27 | -0.35 |
| Singapore | -41.39 | -2.33 | -12.09 | -0.41 |
| Spain | -40.24 | -2.27 | -11.43 | -0.39 |
| Sri Lanka | -41.55 | -2.34 | -11.87 | -0.40 |
| Sweden | -41.31 | -2.33 | -12.85 | -0.44 |
| Switzerland | -41.26 | -2.33 | -12.64 | -0.43 |
| Syria | -41.95 | -2.37 | -14.36 | -0.49 |
| Tanzania | -41.01 | -2.31 | -11.93 | -0.40 |
| Thailand | -40.49 | -2.29 | -11.07 | -0.38 |
| Trinidad | -43.01 | -2.41 | -13.63 | -0.46 |
| Tunisia | -41.47 | -2.34 | -13.70 | -0.46 |
| Turkey | -40.37 | -2.28 | -12.05 | -0.41 |
| U.K. | -39.49 | -2.23 | -10.86 | -0.37 |
| W. Germany | -39.47 | -2.24 | -10.84 | -0.37 |
| Yugoslavia | -40.89 | -2.31 | -12.78 | -0.44 |
| Zimbabwe | -42.60 | -2.40 | -13.06 | -0.44 |

Table 19

Country-Specific Intercepts: Consumer Trade Equations

| | Consumer | | | |
| | Exports | | Imports | |
| Country | Est. | *t*-val. | Est. | *t*-val. |
|---|---|---|---|---|
| Australia | -60.61 | -2.97 | 16.08 | 0.48 |
| Austria | -61.67 | -3.03 | 15.68 | 0.47 |
| Brazil | -59.07 | -2.90 | 15.58 | 0.47 |
| Canada | -59.32 | -2.91 | 16.67 | 0.50 |
| Colombia | -60.42 | -2.96 | 15.19 | 0.45 |
| Cyprus | -63.75 | -3.11 | 15.14 | 0.45 |
| Denmark | -61.93 | -3.03 | 16.04 | 0.48 |
| El Salvador | -61.97 | -3.03 | 15.50 | 0.46 |
| Ethiopia | -60.69 | -2.98 | 14.30 | 0.43 |
| Finland | -62.07 | -3.04 | 15.57 | 0.46 |
| France | -59.66 | -2.93 | 15.96 | 0.48 |
| Greece | -61.64 | -3.02 | 15.28 | 0.46 |
| Hungary | -61.58 | -3.02 | 15.13 | 0.45 |
| Iceland | -64.39 | -3.13 | 15.93 | 0.47 |
| India | -58.00 | -2.85 | 15.31 | 0.46 |
| Ireland | -62.14 | -3.04 | 15.67 | 0.47 |
| Israel | -61.62 | -3.01 | 16.16 | 0.48 |
| Italy | -59.83 | -2.94 | 15.91 | 0.48 |
| Japan | -58.84 | -2.89 | 15.51 | 0.49 |
| Jordan | -62.38 | -3.05 | 14.13 | 0.42 |
| Kenya | -61.35 | -3.00 | 14.66 | 0.44 |
| Malaysia | -60.51 | -2.96 | 16.31 | 0.49 |
| Malta | -64.52 | -3.14 | 15.25 | 0.45 |
| Morocco | -60.84 | -2.99 | 14.60 | 0.44 |
| Netherlands | -60.56 | -2.97 | 15.88 | 0.47 |
| New Zealand | -62.26 | -3.04 | 16.34 | 0.49 |
| Nicaragua | -62.41 | -3.05 | 15.54 | 0.46 |
| Norway | -62.02 | -3.04 | 15.66 | 0.47 |

(continued)

| Country | Consumer Exports Est. | *t*-val. | Consumer Imports Est. | *t*-val. |
|---|---|---|---|---|
| Pakistan | -59.80 | -2.94 | 14.84 | 0.44 |
| Philippines | -59.88 | -2.94 | 15.54 | 0.46 |
| S. Africa | -60.29 | -2.96 | 15.72 | 0.47 |
| S. Korea | -59.99 | -2.94 | 16.27 | 0.49 |
| Singapore | -61.37 | -3.00 | 17.09 | 0.51 |
| Spain | -60.28 | -2.96 | 15.77 | 0.47 |
| Sri Lanka | -61.68 | -3.02 | 15.46 | 0.47 |
| Sweden | -61.28 | -3.01 | 16.12 | 0.48 |
| Switzerland | -61.29 | -3.00 | 16.11 | 0.48 |
| Syria | -61.73 | -3.02 | 14.07 | 0.42 |
| Tanzania | -60.79 | -2.98 | 14.62 | 0.44 |
| Thailand | -60.25 | -2.96 | 15.51 | 0.46 |
| Trinidad | -63.20 | -3.08 | 14.77 | 0.44 |
| Tunisia | -61.65 | -3.02 | 14.61 | 0.44 |
| Turkey | -60.22 | -2.96 | 14.68 | 0.44 |
| U.K. | -59.38 | -2.92 | 15.92 | 0.48 |
| W. Germany | -59.36 | -2.92 | 15.20 | 0.49 |
| Yugoslavia | -60.86 | -2.99 | 15.35 | 0.46 |
| Zimbabwe | -62.37 | -3.05 | 14.16 | 0.42 |

Table 20

Country-Specific Intercepts: Producer Trade Equations

| Country | Producer | | | |
| | Exports | | Imports | |
| | Est. | *t*-val. | Est. | *t*-val. |
| --- | --- | --- | --- | --- |
| Australia | -47.60 | -2.05 | -111.11 | -2.15 |
| Austria | -49.16 | -2.12 | -112.49 | -2.18 |
| Brazil | -45.72 | -1.97 | -109.49 | -2.12 |
| Canada | -46.49 | -2.00 | -109.30 | -2.12 |
| Colombia | -47.62 | -2.05 | -112.49 | -2.17 |
| Cyprus | -52.08 | -2.23 | -117.43 | -2.25 |
| Denmark | -49.43 | -2.13 | -112.33 | -2.17 |
| El Salvador | -49.69 | -2.13 | -114.65 | -2.21 |
| Ethiopia | -48.06 | -2.07 | -117.83 | -2.27 |
| Finland | -49.65 | -2.14 | -112.09 | -2.16 |
| France | -46.46 | -2.01 | -109.53 | -2.12 |
| Greece | -48.96 | -2.11 | -112.95 | -2.18 |
| Hungary | -49.41 | -2.13 | -113.80 | -2.20 |
| Iceland | -52.93 | -2.26 | -116.58 | -2.23 |
| India | -44.18 | -1.91 | -110.95 | -2.15 |
| Ireland | -49.41 | -2.12 | -113.12 | -2.18 |
| Israel | -49.04 | -2.10 | -112.92 | -2.17 |
| Italy | -46.60 | -2.01 | -109.76 | -2.13 |
| Japan | -45.58 | -1.97 | -108.39 | -2.10 |
| Jordan | -50.12 | -2.15 | -117.50 | -2.26 |
| Kenya | -48.70 | -2.09 | -115.35 | -2.22 |
| Malaysia | -48.20 | -2.07 | -112.68 | -2.17 |
| Malta | -52.66 | -2.25 | -118.14 | -2.26 |
| Morocco | -48.39 | -2.09 | -114.62 | -2.21 |
| Netherlands | -47.52 | -2.05 | -110.81 | -2.14 |
| New Zealand | -49.53 | -2.13 | -113.49 | -2.18 |
| Nicaragua | -50.15 | -2.15 | -115.33 | -2.22 |
| Norway | -49.48 | -2.13 | -112.61 | -2.17 |

(continued)

| Country | Producer Exports Est. | Exports *t*-val. | Imports Est. | Imports *t*-val. |
|---------|------|--------|---------|--------|
| Pakistan | -46.78 | -2.02 | -112.10 | -2.17 |
| Philippines | -47.11 | -2.03 | -113.02 | -2.19 |
| S. Africa | -47.19 | -2.03 | -111.09 | -2.14 |
| S. Korea | -47.23 | -2.03 | -111.54 | -2.15 |
| Singapore | -48.80 | -2.09 | -112.57 | -2.16 |
| Spain | -47.24 | -2.04 | -110.83 | -2.14 |
| Sri Lanka | -47.13 | -2.11 | -114.93 | -2.21 |
| Sweden | -48.57 | -2.09 | -111.37 | -2.15 |
| Switzerland | -48.71 | -2.10 | -111.24 | -2.15 |
| Syria | -49.53 | -2.13 | -115.59 | -2.23 |
| Tanzania | -48.34 | -2.08 | -113.89 | -2.19 |
| Thailand | -47.50 | -2.05 | -113.09 | -2.18 |
| Trinidad | -50.90 | -2.18 | -113.44 | -2.18 |
| Tunisia | -49.07 | -2.11 | -114.28 | -2.20 |
| Turkey | -47.23 | -2.04 | -112.78 | -2.18 |
| U.K. | -46.16 | -1.99 | -109.55 | -2.12 |
| W. Germany | -46.21 | -2.00 | -109.17 | -2.12 |
| Yugoslavia | -48.08 | -2.07 | -112.24 | -2.17 |
| Zimbabwe | -50.17 | -2.16 | -113.16 | -2.18 |

# References

Anderson, James E., "A Theoretical Foundation for the Gravity Equation," *American Economic Review* 69 (1979), 106-116.

Bergstrand, Jeffrey H., "The Gravity Equation in International Trade: Some Microeconomic Foundations and Empirical Evidence," *Review of Economics and Statistics* 67 (1985), 474-481.

Berry, R. Albert, and Ronald Soligo, "Some Welfare Aspects of International Migration," *Journal of Political Economy* 77 (1969), 778-794.

Bhagwati, Jagdish N., "International Factor Movements and National Advantage," *Indian Economic Review* 14 (1979), 73.

Bhagwati, Jagdish N., and K. Hamada, "The Brain Drain, International Integration of Markets for Professionals and Unemployment," *Journal of Development Economics* 1 (1974), 19.

Bhagwati, Jagdish N., and Carlos Alfredo Rodriguez, "Welfare-Theoretical Analyses of the Brain Drain," *Journal of Development Economics* 2 (1975), 195-221.

Borjas, George J., *Friends or Strangers: The Impact of Immigrants on the U.S. Economy* (New York: Basic Books, 1990).

Boyd, M., "Family and Personal Networks in International Migration: Recent Developments and New Agendas," *International Migration Review* 23 (1989), 638.

Cornelius, W., "Mexican Immigrants in California Today," in Institute of Social Science Research, *ISSR Working Papers*, 5 (10), University of California, Los Angeles (1990).

DeFreitas, Gregory, "Hispanic Immigration and Labor Market Segmentation," *Industrial Relations* 27 (2, 1988), 195-214.

Dixit, Avinash K., and V. Norman, *Theory of International Trade* (Cambridge: Cambridge University Press, 1980)

Dixit, Avinash K., and Joseph E. Stiglitz, "Monopolistic Competition and Optimum Product Diversity," *American Economic Review* 67 (1977) 297-308.

Edwards, Sebastian, "Terms of Trade, Tariffs, and Labor Market Adjustment in Developing Countries," *The World Bank Economic Review* 2, no. 2, (1988).

Edwards, Sebastian, "Anticipated Protectionist Policies, Real Exchange Rates, and the Current Account," *NBER Working Papers*, no. 2214 (1987).

Ethier, W., "International Trade and Labor Migration," *American Economic Review* 75 (1985), 691.

Fomby, Thomas B., R. Carter Hill, and Stanley R. Johnson, *Advanced Econometric Methods* (New York: Springer-Verlag, 1984).

Gould, David Michael, "Immigrant Links to the Home Country: Empirical Implications for U.S. Bilateral Trade Flows," *Review of Economics and Statistics* 76 (2) (1994), 302-16.

Greenwood, Michael, and J. McDowell, "Factor Market Consequences of U.S. Poor to Rich Immigration," *Journal of Economic Literature* December (1985).

Greenwood, Michael, "The Economics of Mass Migration from Poor to Rich Countries," *AEA Papers and Proceedings* 73 (1983), 173.

Grossman, Gene M., and Elhanan Helpman, *Innovation and Growth in the Global Economy* (Cambridge: MIT Press, 1991).

Grossman, J., "The Substitutability of Natives and Immigrants in Production," *Review of Economics and Statistics* 64 (1982), 596.

Grubel, Herbert B., and Anthony C. Scott, "The International Flow of Human Capital," *American Economic Review* 56 (1966), 268-283.

Harvey, Andrew C., *The Econometric Analysis of Time Series* (Oxford: Philip Allan Publishers Ltd., 1981).

Helpman, Elhanan, and Paul R. Krugman, *Market Structure and Foreign Trade: Increasing Returns, Imperfect Competition, and the International Economy* (Cambridge: MIT Press, 1985).

Johnson, Harry G., "Some Economic Aspects of the Brain Drain," *Pakistani Development Review* 7 (1967), 379-415.

Jones, Ronald, "A Three-factor Model in Theory, Trade, and History," in *Trade, Balance of Payments, and Growth*, ed. Bhagwati, Jones, Mundell and Vanek (Amsterdam: North-Holland, 1971).

Jovanovic, Boyan, and Rafael Rob, "The Growth and Diffusion of Knowledge," *Review of Economic Studies* 56 (1989), 569-582.

Keely, C., and P. Elwell, "International Migration: Canada and the United States" in *Global Trends in Migration*, ed. Kritz, Keely, Tomasi (New York: The Center for Migration Studies of New York, 1981), 181.

Leamer, Edward E., "Talent in a General Equilibrium Model," (University of California, Los Angeles, Mimeo. (1990).

Leamer, Edward E., "Theory and Evidence of Immigrant Enclaves," University of California, Los Angeles, *UCLA Working Papers* (1988).

Light, Ivan, and Edna Bonacich, *Immigrant Entrepreneurs* (Berkeley: University of California Press, 1988).

Light, Ivan.,"Ethnicity and Business Enterprise," in *Making It in America*, ed. Stolarik, M. Mark and Murray Friedman (Lewisburg, Penn.: Bucknell University, 1985).

Light, Ivan., P. Bhachu, and S. Karageorgis, "Migration Networks and Immigrant Entrepreneurship," in Institute of Social Science Research, *ISSR Working Papers*, University of California, Los Angeles (1990).

Lucus, Robert E., Jr., "On the Mechanics of Economic Development," *Journal of Monetary Economics* 22 (1988), 3-42.

Massey, D., "Economic Development and International Migration in Comparative Perspective," *Population and Development Review* 14 (1988), 383.

Markusen, James, "Factor Movements and Commodity Trade as Complements," *Journal of International Economics* 14 (1983), 341.

Markusen, James, and L. Svensson, "Trade in Goods and Factors with International Differences in Technology," *International Economic Review* 26 (1985), 175.

Mayer, Wolfgang, "Short-Run and Long-Run Equilibrium for a Small Open Economy," *Journal of Political Economy* 82 (5) (1974), 955.

Min, Pyong Gap, "Korean Immigrants in Los Angeles," in Institute of Social Science Research, *ISSR Working Papers*, 2 (2), University of California, Los Angeles (1990).

Mundell, Robert, "International Trade and Factor Mobility." *American Economic Review* 97 (1957), 321.

Mussa, Michael, "Tariffs and Distribution of Income: Importance of Factor Specificity, Substitutability, and Intensity in Short and Long Run," *Journal of Political Economy* 82 (6) (1974), 1191.

Ohlin, B., *Interregional and International Trade.*(Cambridge: Harvard University Press, 1933).

Papademetriou, D., "U.S. Legal Immigration Reform: Issues and Challenges," in Institute of Social Science Research, *ISSR Working Papers*, 5 (17), University of California, Los Angeles (1990).

Powell, Alan A., and F.H.G. Gruen, "The Constant Elasticity of Transformation Production Frontier and Linear Supply System,"*International Economic Review* 9 (1968), 315-328.

Purvis, D., "Technology, Trade, and Factor Mobility," *Economic Journal* 82 (1972), 991.

Rauch, James E., "Reconciling the Pattern of Trade with the Pattern of Migration," *American Economic Review* 81 (1991), 775-796.

Razin, Eran, "Immigrant Entrepreneurs in Israel, Canada, and California," in Institute of Social Science Research, *ISSR Working Papers*, 5 (15), University of California, Los Angeles (1990).

Reubens, E., "International Migration Models and Policies," *AEA Papers and Proceedings* 73 (2) (1983), 178.

Romer, Paul M., "Endogenous Growth and Technical Change," *Journal of Political Economy* 98 (1990), 71-102.

Ruffin, Roy J., "International Factor Movements," in *Handbook of International Economics, vol. 1,* eds. Jones, Ronald and Peter Kenen (Amsterdam: Elsevier Science Publishers, B.V., 1984).

Samuelson, Paul, "International Factor-Price Equalization Once Again," *Economic Journal* 59 (1949), 181.

Samuelson, Paul, "International Trade and Equalization of Factor Price," *Economic Journal* 58 (1948), 163.

Tobin, James, "Notes on the Economic Theory of Expulsion and Expropriation." *Journal of Development Economics* 1 (1974), 7.

Topel, Robert J., and Robert H. LaLonde, "Labor Market Adjustments to Increased Immigration," in *Immigration, Trade and the Labor Market,* eds. Abowd, John M., and Richard B. Freeman (Chicago: University of Chicago Press, 1991).

Wong, Kar-Yiu, "Are International Trade and Factor Mobility Substitutes?" *Journal of International Economics* 21 (1986a), 25-43.

Wong, Kar-Yiu, "International Factor Mobility and the Volume of Trade: An Empirical Study," paper presented at the NBER Conference on Empirical Methods for International Trade, Cambridge (1986b).

Zubrzycki, J., "International Migration in Australasia and the South Pacific," in *Global Trends in Migration,* eds. Kritz, Keely, and Tomasi (New York: The Center for Migration Studies of New York, 1981), 158.

# Index